THE SHADOW OF A GUNMAN

A Tragedy in Two Acts

BY
SEAN O'CASEY

S A M U E L   F R E N C H

LONDON

NEW YORK   TORONTO   SYDNEY   HOLLYWOOD

PRINTED AND BOUND IN GREAT BRITAIN BY
BUTLER & TANNER LTD, FROME AND LONDON

THE SHADOW OF A GUNMAN

ACT I

SCENE.—*Room in a tenement house in Hilljoy Square. Upstage,* L. *wall, a small window. On the* R. *a door.* C. *back, a large window curtained with shabby lace curtains. To* R. *of window a washhand-stand with basin ; in basin a jug containing water, a dirty towel over jug. To* L. *of window a dresser, with crockery. On the* L. *wall is the fireplace. In room are two beds, one to the* R. *of window having its head towards* C. *of stage ; the other* L. *of window with its head to back of stage.* L.C. *downstage is a table. On the table are a vase containing wild flowers, a few books, writing materials and a typewriter charged for work. Beside table a chair facing typewriter. Another chair in front of bed* R. *on which clothes are hanging over back. At the head of this bed a large suitcase filled with bundles of knives, forks, spoons, braces, etc. On mantelpiece, above fireplace, is a statue of the Sacred Heart, and a small crucifix and a candle in candlestick.*

See Ground Plan of Scene.

DAVOREN *is sitting at the table typing. He is about* 30. *There is in his face an expression that seems to indicate an eternal war between weakness and strength ; there is in the lines of the brow and chin an indication of a desire for activity, while in his eyes there is visible an unquenchable tendency towards rest. His struggle through life has been a hard one, and his efforts have been handicapped by an inherited and self-developed devotion to "the might of design, the mystery of colour and the belief in the redemption of all things by beauty everlasting." His life would drive him mad were it not for the fact that he never knew any other. He bears upon his body the marks of the struggle for existence and the efforts towards self-expression.*

SEUMAS SHIELDS, *who is in the bed to the right, is a heavily built man of* 35 *; he is dark-haired and sallow-complexioned. In him is frequently manifested the superstition, the fear and the malignity of primitive man.*

DAVOREN (*lilting an air as he composes*). Or when sweet Summer's ardent arms outspread

5

Entwined with flowers,
Enfold us, like two lovers newly wed,
Thro' ravish'd hours—
Then sorrow, woe and pain lose all their powers,
For each is dead, and life is only ours.

(*Loud knocking at the door* R.)

VOICE OF WOMAN (*at door outside*). Are you awake, Mr. Shields —Mr. Shields, are you awake ? Are you goin' to get up to-day at all, at all ?

(*A pause.*)

(*Outside the door* R.) Mr. Shields, is there any use of callin' you at all ? This is a nice nine o'clock : do you know what time it is, Mr. Shields ?

SEUMAS (*loudly*). Yus !

VOICE (*outside the door* R.). Why don't you get up, then, an' not have the house turned into a bedlam tryin' to waken you ?

SEUMAS (*shouting*). All right, all right, all right ! The way these oul' ones bawl at a body ! Upon my soul ! I'm beginnin' to believe that the Irish People are still in the STONE AGE. If they could they'd throw a bomb at you.

DAVOREN. A land mine exploding under the bed is the only thing that would lift you out of it.

SEUMAS (*stretching himself*). Oh-h-h. I was fast in the arms of Morpheus—he was one of the infernal deities, son of Somnos, wasn't he ?

DAVOREN. I think so.

SEUMAS. The poppy was his emblem, wasn't it ?

DAVOREN. Ah, I don't know.

SEUMAS. It's a bit cold this morning, I think, isn't it ?

DAVOREN (*with a movement of annoyance*). It's quite plain I'm not going to get much quietness in this house.

SEUMAS (*after a pause*). I wonder what time is it ?

DAVOREN. The Angelus went some time ago.

(*This information stuns* SEUMAS. *He lies flat for a moment, then springs into a sitting position, with a look of consternation on his face.*)

SEUMAS. The Angelus ! It couldn't be that late, could it ? I asked them to call me at nine, so that I could get Mass before I went on me rounds. Why didn't *you* give us a rap ?

DAVOREN (*looking at* SEUMAS). Give you a rap ! Why, man, they've been thundering at the door and hammering at the window for the past two hours, till the house shook to its very foundations, but you took less notice of the infernal din than I would take of the strumming of a grasshopper.

SEUMAS (*surlily*). There's no fear of you thinking of anyone else when you're at your poetry. The land of Saints and Scholars 'ill shortly be a land of bloody poets.

(SEUMAS *slides angrily out of the bed at back, sits on bed with back to audience, and begins to pull on his trousers.* DAVOREN *goes on composing. As* SEUMAS *pulls his trousers up, he finds the back is to the front; with a movement of annoyance, he takes them off, and puts them right way on.*)

(*Anxiously.*) I suppose Maguire has come an' gone ?

DAVOREN (*looking over at* SEUMAS). Maguire ? No, he hasn't been here—why, did you expect him ?

SEUMAS (*in a burst of indignation, as he fixes his braces*). He said he'd be here at nine ; " Before the last chime has sthruck," says he, " I'll be comin' in on the door," an' it must be—what time is it now ?

DAVOREN. Oh, it must be half-past twelve.

SEUMAS. Did anybody ever see the like of the Irish People ? Is there any use of tryin' to do anything in this country ? Have everything packed and ready, have everything packed and ready, have . . .

DAVOREN. And have you everything packed and ready ?

SEUMAS. What's the use of having anything packed and ready when he didn't come ? No wonder this unfortunate country is as it is, for you can't depend upon the word of a single individual in it. I suppose he was too damn lazy to get up ; he wanted the streets to be well aired first. Oh, Kathleen Ni Houlihan, your way's a thorny way.

(SEUMAS *comes forward,* R. *end of bed, and sits down on chair, front,* R. *end of bed, and laces his boots.*)

DAVOREN. Ah me ! alas, pain, pain ever, for ever !

SEUMAS. That's from Shelley's *Prometheus Unbound.* I could never agree with Shelley, not that there's anything to be said against him as a poet—as a poet—but . . .

DAVOREN. He flung a few stones through stained-glass windows.

SEUMAS. He wasn't the first nor he won't be the last to do that, but the stained-glass windows—more than ever of them—are here still, and Shelley is doing a jazz dance down below.

(SEUMAS *laughs ironically, and* DAVOREN *looks up from his work with a shocked expression on his face.*)

DAVOREN (*shocked*). And you actually rejoice and are exceedingly glad that, as you believe, Shelley, the sensitive, high-minded, noble-hearted Shelley, is suffering the tortures of the damned.

SEUMAS. I rejoice in the vindication of the Church and Truth.

DAVOREN. Bah. You know as little about truth as anybody else, and you care as little about the Church as the least of those that profess her faith ; your religion is simply the state of being afraid that God will torture your soul in the next world as you are afraid the Black and Tans will torture your body in this.

(SEUMAS *gets up from chair, goes round* L. *end of his bed, to washstand back,* R. *He is now wearing trousers, boots, and waistcoat. He takes jug out of basin, pours some water into basin, leaves jug on floor under washstand.*)

SEUMAS. Go on, me boy ; I'll have a right laugh at you when both of us are dead.

DAVOREN. You're welcome to laugh as much as you like at me, when both of us are dead.

SEUMAS (*thinking a moment beside washstand*). I don't think I need to wash myself this morning. (*To* DAVOREN.) Do I look all right ?

DAVOREN. You're all right ; it's too late, now, to start washing yourself. Didn't you wash yourself yesterday morning ?

SEUMAS. Oh, I gave meself a great rub yesterday.

(SEUMAS *takes up suitcase from floor,* L. *end of bed, brings it to front of bed, and places it on chair, front of his bed. He opens case and arranges the packages in the case. Takes out some braces.*)

I think I'll bring out a few of the braces too ; damn it, they're well worth sixpence each ; there's great stuff in them—did you see them ?

DAVOREN. Yes, you showed them to me before.

SEUMAS. They're great value ; I only hope I'll be able to get enough o' them. I'm wearing a pair of them meself—

(SEUMAS *walks over with a pair of braces in his hand, to table* R., *bends over to show them to* DAVOREN.)

They'd do Samson, they're so strong.

(*He goes back to case and begins to count the spoons.*)

There's a dozen in each of these parcels—three, six, nine—damn it, there's only eleven in this one. I better try another. Three, six, nine—my God, there's only eleven in this one too, and one of them bent ! Now I suppose I'll have to go through the whole bloody lot of them, for I'd never be easy in me mind thinkin' there'd be more than a dozen in some o' them. And still we're looking for freedom— ye gods, it's a glorious country ! (*He lets one fall, which he stoops to pick up and his braces snap.*) Oh, my God, there's the braces after breakin'.

DAVOREN (*laughing*). That doesn't look as if they were strong enough for Samson.

SEUMAS (*apologizing for braces*). I put a heavy strain on them too sudden. There's that fella, Maguire, never turned up, either— he's almost too lazy to wash himself.

(*As* SEUMAS *is mending the broken brace,* MAGUIRE *rushes in by door* R. *He carries a handbag.*)

(*To* Maguire *in a burst of anger.*) This is a nice nine o'clock. What's the use of you coming at this hour o' the day ? Do you think we're going to work be moonlight ? If you weren't goin' to come at nine couldn't you say you weren't. . . .

Maguire (R.). Keep your hair on ; I just blew in to tell you that I couldn't go to-day at all. I have to go to Knocksedan.

Seumas (*at head of bed*, R.). Knocksedan ! An' what, in the name o' God, is bringin' you to Knocksedan ?

Maguire. Business, business. I'm going out to catch butterflies.

Seumas (*angrily*). If you want to make a cod of anybody, make a cod of somebody else, an' don't be tryin' to make a cod o' me. Here I've had everything packed an' ready for hours ; you were to be here at nine, an' you wait till just one o'clock to come rushin' in like a mad bull to say you've got to go to Knocksedan ! Can't you leave Knocksedan till to-morrow ?

Maguire (*flippantly*). Can't be did, can't be did, Seumas ; if I waited till to-morrow all the butterflies might be dead. I'll leave this bag here till this evening.

(*He slips over to* Seumas's *bed*, R., *and puts the handbag under it with a quick movement. He slips back to door*, R., *opens it and goes out almost before the other two are aware of it.*)

(*Going out door*, R.). Good . . . bye . . . eee !

Seumas (*with a gesture of despair*). Oh, this is a hopeless country ! There's a fellow that thinks that the four cardinal virtues are not to be found outside an Irish Republic. I don't want to boast about myself—I don't want to boast about myself, and I suppose I could call meself as good a Gael as some of those that are knocking about now—knocking about now—as good a Gael as some that are knocking about now,—but I remember the time when I taught Irish six nights a week, when in the Irish Republican Brotherhood I payed me rifle levy like a man, an' when the Church refused to have anything to do with James Stephens, I tarred a prayer for the repose of his soul on the steps of the Pro-Cathedral. Now, after all me work for Dark Rosaleen, the only answer you can get from a roarin' Republican to a simple question is " good-by . . . ee."

(Seumas *turns and looks at* Davoren *inquiringly.*)

Now, what in the name o' God can be bringin' him to Knocksedan ?

Davoren (*ironically*). Hadn't you betther run out, an' ask him ?

(Seumas, *still standing by chair, front*, R. *end of his bed, begins to pack his case vigorously.*)

Seumas. That's right, that's right—make a joke about it ! That's the Irish People all over—they treat a joke as a serious thing and a serious thing as a joke. Upon me soul, I'm beginning to believe that the Irish People aren't, never were an' never will be fit for self-government. They've made Balor of the Evil Eye King of

Ireland, an' so signs on it there's neither conscience nor honesty from one end of the country to the other. Well, I hope he'll have a happy day in Knocksedan.

(*A knock is heard at door*, R.)

(*Looking towards door*, R.). Who's that?

(*Another knock, a little louder.*)

(*Staring at door, irritably.*) Who's that? Who's there?
DAVOREN (*irritably, over to* SEUMAS). Damn it, man, can't you go and see!

(SEUMAS *goes over and opens the door. A man of about* 60 *is revealed, dressed in a faded blue serge suit; a half-tall hat is on his head. It is evident that he has no love for* SEUMAS, *who denies him the deference he believes is due from a tenant to a landlord. He carries some papers in his hand.*)

THE LANDLORD (*ironically coming into room a little*, R.). Good day, Mr. Shields; it's meself that hopes you're feelin' well—you're lookin' well, anyhow—though you can't always go be looks nowadays.
SEUMAS (L. *of* LANDLORD). It doesn't matter whether I'm looking well or feelin' well; I'm all right, thanks be to God.
THE LANDLORD. I'm very glad to hear it.
SEUMAS. It doesn't matter whether you're glad to hear it or not, Mr. Mulligan.
THE LANDLORD. You're not inclined to be very civil, Mr. Shields.
SEUMAS. Look here, Mr. Mulligan, if you come here to raise an argument, I've something to do—let me tell you that.
THE LANDLORD. I don't come here to raise no argument; a person ud have small gains argufyin' with you—let me tell you that.

(SEUMAS *catches* LANDLORD *by an arm, and tries to get him nearer the door*, R. THE LANDLORD *breaks away. This isn't a rough movement, but suggestive of both their thoughts.* SEUMAS *makes a motion to shut the door*, R.)

SEUMAS. I've no time to be standin' here gostherin' with you—let me shut the door, Mr. Mulligan.
THE LANDLORD. You'll not shut no door till you've heard what I've got to say.
SEUMAS. Well, say it then, an' go about your business.
THE LANDLORD. You're very high an' mighty, but take care you're not goin' to get a drop. What a baby you are not to know what brings me here. Maybe you thought I was goin' to ask you to come to tea.
DAVOREN (*to himself*). Ah me! alas, pain, pain ever, for ever!
SEUMAS (*roughly*). Are you goin' to let me shut the door, Mr. Mulligan?

THE LANDLORD. I'm here for me rent ; you don't like the idea of bein' asked to pay your just an' lawful debts.

SEUMAS (*indignantly*). You'll get your rent when you learn to keep your rent-book in a proper way.

THE LANDLORD. I'm not goin' to take any lessons from you, anyhow.

SEUMAS. I want to have no more talk with you, Mr. Mulligan.

THE LANDLORD. Talk or no talk, you owe me eleven weeks' rent, an' it's marked down again' you in black an' white.

SEUMAS (*loudly*). I don't care a damn if it was marked down in green, white an' yellow.

THE LANDLORD. You're a terribly independent fellow, an' it ud be fitter for you to be less funny an' stop tryin' to be billickin' honest an' respectable people.

SEUMAS (*warningly*). Just you be careful what you're sayin', Mr. Mulligan. There's law in the land still.

THE LANDLORD. Be me sowl there is, an' you're goin' to get a little of it now. (*He offers the papers to* SEUMAS.) Them's for you.

SEUMAS (*hesitating to take them and pushing* LANDLORD'S *hand away*). I want to have nothing to do with you, Mr. Mulligan.

THE LANDLORD (*throwing the papers in the* C. *of the room*). What am I better ? It was the sorry day I ever let you come into this house. Maybe them notices to quit will stop your writin' letters to the papers about me an' me house.

DAVOREN (*disgusted*). For goodness' sake, bring the man in, and don't be discussing the situation like a pair of primitive troglodytes.

SEUMAS (*taking no notice of* DAVOREN). Writing letters to the papers is my business, an' I'll write as often as I like, when I like an' how I like.

THE LANDLORD. You'll not write about this house at all events. You can blow about the state of the yard, but you took care to say nothin' about payin' rent : oh no, that's not in your line. But since you're not staisfied with the house you can pack up an' go to another.

SEUMAS. I'll go, Mr. Mulligan, when I think fit, an' no sooner.

THE LANDLORD. Not content with keeping the rent, you're startin' to bring in lodgers—(*to* DAVOREN) not that I'm sayin' anythin' again' you, sir. Bringin' in lodgers without as much as be your leave—what's the world comin' to at all that a man's house isn't his own ? But I'll soon put a stop to your gallop, for on the twenty-eight of the next month out you go, an' there'll be few sorry to see your back.

SEUMAS. I'll go when I like.

THE LANDLORD (*turning towards* R. *to go*). I'll let you see whether you own the house or no.

SEUMAS. I'll go when I like !

THE LANDLORD. We'll see about that.

SEUMAS. We'll see.

THE LANDLORD (*turning to give a last angry look at* SEUMAS).   Ay, we'll see.

(THE LANDLORD *goes out and* SEUMAS *bangs the door* R. *shut.*)

(*Outside.*)   Mind you, I'm in earnest ; you'll not stop in this house a minute longer than the twenty-eight.
SEUMAS (*with a roar*).   Ah, go to hell !

(SEUMAS *goes back to chair* R. *front of his bed, and recommences packing his suitcase.* DAVOREN, *in an irritated mood, gets up from his chair and walks about down and upstage, front of fireplace.*)

DAVOREN (*pacing about*).   What in the name of God persuaded me to come to such a house as this !

(SEUMAS *takes coat and muffler from back of chair, and puts both on.*)

SEUMAS.   It's nothing when you're used to it ; you're too thin-skinned altogether.   The oul' sod's got the wind up about you, that's all.
DAVOREN.   Got the wind up about me !
SEUMAS.   He thinks you're on the run.   He's afraid of a raid, and that his lovely property'll be destroyed.

(SEUMAS *shuts suitcase, and comes downstage towards door,* R.   *He halts a little to* L. *of door,* R.)

Sure they all think you're on the run.   Mrs. Henderson thinks it, Tommy Owens thinks it, Mrs. an' Mr. Grigson think it, an' Minnie Powell thinks it too.   (*Picking up his attaché case.*)   I'd better be off if I'm goin' to do anything to-day.
DAVOREN.   What are we going to do with these notices to quit ?
SEUMAS (*carelessly*).   Oh, shove them up on the mantelpiece behind one of the statues.
DAVOREN.   Oh, I mean what action shall we take ?
SEUMAS.   I haven't time to stop now.   We'll talk about them when I come back. . . .   I'll get me own back on that oul' Mulligan yet.   I wish to God they would come an' smash his old rookery to pieces, for it's all he thinks of ; and, mind you, old Mulligan would call himself a descendant of the thrue Gaels of Ireland—

Oh, proud were the Chieftains of famed Inisfail,
The stars, of our sky an the salt of our soil—

(*Sarcastically.*)   Oh, Kathleen Ni Houlihan, your way's a thorny way !   (*He goes out by door,* R.)

(DAVOREN *crosses by back of table to* C. *of stage, picks up papers flung on floor by* LANDLORD ; *goes back,* L., *and puts them behind statue. He returns to table and sits down at typewriter.*)

DAVOREN (*with self-pity*).   Oh, Donal Og O'Davoren, your way's a thorny way.   Your last state is worse than your first.   Ah me, alas !   Pain, pain ever, for ever.   Like thee, Prometheus, no change, no pause, no hope.   Ah, life, life, life !

(*There is a gentle knock at the door.   DAVOREN looks towards door R.*)

Another Fury come to plague me now !
    DAVOREN.   You can knock till you're tired.

(*The door R. opens and MINNIE POWELL enters with an easy confidence one would not expect her to possess from her gentle way of knocking. She is a girl of 23, but the fact of being forced to earn her living, and to take care of herself, on account of her parents' early death, has given her a force and an assurance beyond her years.   She has lost the sense of fear (she does not know this), and, consequently, she is at ease in all places and before all persons, even those of a superior education, so long as she meets them in the atmosphere that surrounds the members of her own class.   Her hair is brown, neither light nor dark, but partaking of both tints according to the light or shade she may happen to be in.   Her well-shaped figure—a rare thing in a city girl—is charmingly dressed in a brown tailor-made costume, her stockings and shoes are a darker brown tint than the costume, and all are crowned by a silk tam o' shanter of a rich blue tint.*)

MINNIE.   Are you in, Mr. Shields ?
    DAVOREN (*rapidly*).   No, he's not, Minnie ; he's just gone out— if you run out quickly you're sure to catch him.
    MINNIE.   Oh, it's all right, Mr. Davoren, you'll do just as well ; I just come in for a drop o' milk for a cup o' tea ; I shouldn't be troublin' you this way, but I'm sure you don't mind.
    DAVOREN (*dubiously*).   No trouble in the world—delighted, I'm sure.

(*He crosses stage, C., between beds, to dresser, gets jug of milk, comes down to MINNIE, C.R., and pours some milk into the jug she has in her hand.*)

(*Pouring milk into jug*).   There, will that be enough ?
    MINNIE.   Plenty, lashins, thanks.

(*DAVOREN returns to dresser, and leaves his jug of milk back on it. He returns to typewriter.   MINNIE stands C.R.*)

(*Over to DAVOREN*).   Do you be all alone all the day, Mr. Davoren ?
    DAVOREN (*ruefully*).   No, indeed ; I wish to God I was.
    MINNIE.   It's not good for you then.   I don't know how you like to be by yourself—I couldn't stick it long.
    DAVOREN (*wearily*).   No ?
    MINNIE.   No, indeed ; (*with rapture*) there's nothin' I'm more fond of than a Hooley.   I was at one last Sunday—I danced rings

round me! Tommy Owens was there—you know Tommy Owens, don't you?

DAVOREN. I can't say I do.

MINNIE. D'ye not? The little fellow that lives with his mother in the two-pair back—(*ecstatically*) he's a gorgeous melodeon player!

DAVOREN. A gifted son of Orpheus, eh?

MINNIE (*who never heard of Orpheus*). You've said it, Mr. Davoren: the son of poor oul' Battie Owens, a weeshy, dawny, bit of a man that was never sober an' was always talkin' politics. Poor man, it killed him in the long run.

(*She goes over stage to* R. *end of table, puts the jug on it and stands there.*)

DAVOREN. A man should always be drunk, Minnie, when he talks politics—it's the only way in which to make them important.

MINNIE. Tommy takes after the oul' fellow, too; he'd talk from morning till night when he has a few jars in him. (*Suddenly; for, like all of her class,* MINNIE *is not able to converse very long on the one subject, and her thoughts spring from one thing to another.*) Poetry is a grand thing, Mr. Davoren, I'd love to be able to write a poem—a lovely poem on Ireland an' the men o' '98.

DAVOREN. Oh, we've had enough of poems, Minnie, about '98, and of Ireland, too.

MINNIE. Oh, there's a thing for a Republican to say! But I know what you mean: it's time to give up the writing an' take to the gun. (*Her roving eye catches sight of the flowers in the vase.*) What's Mr. Shields doin' with the oul' weeds?

DAVOREN. Those aren't Shields's, they're mine.

(*He comes to front of table, and touches the flowers gently.*)

Wild flowers is a kindlier name for them, Minnie, than weeds. These are wild violets, this is an *Arum maculatum*, or Wake Robin, and these are Celandines, a very beautiful flower related to the buttercups. (*He quotes*):

> One day, when Morn's half-open'd eyes
> Were bright with Spring sunshine—
> My hand was clasp'd in yours, dear love,
> And yours was clasp'd in mine—
> We bow'd as worshippers before
> The Golden Celandine.

MINNIE. Oh, aren't they lovely; an' isn't the poem lovely, too. (*Sitting up on* R. *end of table, facing audience.*) I wonder now, who she was?

DAVOREN (*sitting on table,* L. *of* MINNIE, *facing audience. Puzzled*). She . . . who?

MINNIE. Why the . . . (*roguishly.*) Oh, be the way you don't know.

DAVOREN. Know? I'm sure I don't know.

MINNIE. It doesn't matter, anyhow—that's your own business; I suppose I don't know her.

DAVOREN. Know her, know whom?

MINNIE (*shyly*). Her whose hand was clasped in yours, an' yours was clasped in hers.

DAVOREN. Oh that—that was simply a poem I quoted about the celandine, that might apply to any girl—to you, for instance.

MINNIE (*greatly relieved, coming over and sitting beside* DAVOREN). But you have a sweetheart, all the same, Mr. Davoren, haven't you?

DAVOREN. I? No, not one, Minnie.

MINNIE. Oh, now, you can tell that to someone else; aren't you a poet an' aren't all the girls fond o' poets?

DAVOREN. That may be, but all the poets aren't fond of girls.

MINNIE. They are in the story-books, ay, and fond of more than one, too. (*With a questioning look.*) Are you fond of them, Mr. Davoren?

DAVOREN. Of course I like girls, Minnie, especially girls who can add to their charms by the way in which they dress, like you, for instance.

MINNIE (*shyly*). Oh, now, you're on for coddin' me, Mr. Davoren.

DAVOREN. No, really, Minnie, I'm not; you are a very charming little girl indeed.

MINNIE. Then if I'm a charmin' little girl, you ought to be able to write a poem about me.

DAVOREN (*who has become susceptible to the attractiveness of* MINNIE, *catching her hand*). And so I will, so I will, Minnie; I have written them about girls not half so pretty as yourself.

MINNIE (*disappointedly*). Ah, I knew you had one, I knew you had one now.

DAVOREN. Nonsense. Every girl a poet writes about isn't his sweetheart; Annie Laurie wasn't the sweetheart of Bobbie Burns.

MINNIE. You needn't tell me she wasn't; "An' for bonnie Annie Laurie I'd lay me down an' die." No man ud lay down an' die for any but a sweetheart, not even for a wife.

DAVOREN. No man, Minnie, willingly dies for anything.

MINNIE. Except for his country, like Robert Emmet.

DAVOREN. Even he would have lived on if he could; he died not to deliver Ireland. The British Government killed him to save the British nation.

MINNIE. You're only jokin' now; you'd die for your country.

DAVOREN. I don't know so much about that.

MINNIE (*vehemently*). You would, you would, you would—I know what you are.

DAVOREN. What am I?

MINNIE (*bending towards him, in a whisper*). A gunman on the run!

DAVOREN (*too pleased to deny it*). Maybe I am, and maybe I'm not.

Minnie. Oh, I know, I know, I know. (*Wonderingly.*) Do you never be afraid ?

Davoren. Afraid ! Afraid of what ?

Minnie. Why, the ambushes of course ; *I'm* all of a tremble when I hear a shot go off, an' what must it be to be in the middle of the firin' ?

Davoren (*delighted at* Minnie's *obvious admiration ; sitting proudly on table, and lighting a cigarette with placid affectation*). I'll admit one does be a little nervous at first, but a fellow gets used to it after a bit, till, at last, a gunman throws a bomb as carelessly as a schoolboy throws a snowball.

Minnie (*fervently*). I wish it was all over, all the same. (*Suddenly, with a tremor in her voice.*) You'll take care of yourself, won't you, won't you, Donal—I mean, Mr. Davoren ?

Davoren (*earnestly*). Call me Donal, Minnie ; we're friends, great friends now—(*putting his arm around her.*) Go on, Minnie, call me Donal, let me hear you say Donal.

(Minnie *slips shyly off the table, goes* c., *looks round room.*)

Minnie (*looking round at* Davoren). The place badly needs a tidying up. (*She walks back to him, looks up at him ; calling him, shyly, by Christian name.*) Donal—there. (*Rapidly, half-afraid of* Davoren's *excited emotions.*) But it really does, it's in an awful state. To-morrow's a half-day, an' I'll run in an' straighten it up a bit.

Davoren (*frightened at the suggestion*). No, no, Minnie, you're too pretty for that sort of work ; besides, the people of the house would be sure to start talking about you.

Minnie. An' do you think Minnie Powell cares whether they'll talk or no ? I've had to push me way through life up to this without help from anyone, an' she's not goin' to ask their leave, now, to do what she wants to do.

(Davoren *slips off the table, comes close to* Minnie, c., *and puts his arm round her.*)

Davoren. My soul within art thou, Minnie ! A pioneer in action as I am a pioneer in thought. The two powers that shall " grasp this sorry scheme of things entire, and mould life nearer to the heart's desire." Lovely little Minnie, and brave as well ; brave little Minnie, and lovely as well !

(*His disengaged hand lifts up her bent head, and he looks earnestly at her ; he is stooping to kiss her when* Tommy Owens *appears at the door, which* Minnie *has left partially open.*)

(*Startled by* Owen's *entry,* Minnie *and* Davoren *break away from each other.* Minnie *takes a few steps to back,* Davoren *to front, of table.* Owen *stands* r.c., *looking from one to the other.*)

(TOMMY *is about 25 years of age. He is small and thin; his words are uttered in a nasal drawl; his voice is husky, due to frequent drinks and perpetual cigarette-smoking. He tries to get rid of the huskiness by an occasional cough.* TOMMY *is a hero-worshipper, and, like many others, he is anxious to be on familiar terms with those whom he thinks are braver than he is himself, and whose approbation he tries to win by an assumption equal to their own. He talks in a staccato manner. He has a few drinks taken—it is too early to be drunk—that make him talkative. He is dressed in a suit of dungarees.*)

TOMMY. I seen nothin'—honest—thought you was learnin' to typewrite—Mr. Davoren teachin' you. I seen nothin' else—s'help me God !

MINNIE. We'd be hard put to it if we minded what you seen, Tommy Owens.

(MINNIE, *with a slight shrug of shoulders, goes to back of table,* L.)

TOMMY. Right, Minnie, Tommy Owens has a heart—Evenin', Mr. Davoren—don't mind me comin' in—I'm Tommy Owens— live up in the two-pair back, workin' in Ross an' Walpole's— Mr. Shields knows me well; you needn't be afraid o' me, Mr. Davoren.

DAVOREN. Why should I be afraid of you, Mr. Owens, or of anybody else ?

(DAVOREN *turns, goes front of table, and stands beside* MINNIE. OWENS, *coming closer, stands* C.)

TOMMY. Why should you, indeed ? We're all friends here— Mr. Shields knows me well—all you've got to say is, " Do you know Tommy Owens ? " an' he'll tell you the sort of a man Tommy Owens is. There's no flies on Tommy—got me ?

MINNIE (*indignantly*). For goodness' sake, Tommy, leave Mr. Davoren alone—he's got enough burgeons on him already.

TOMMY. Not a word, Minnie, not a word—Mr. Davoren understands me well, as man to man. It's " Up the Republic " all the time—eh, Mr. Davoren ?

DAVOREN. I know nothing about the Republic ; I have no connection with the politics of the day, and I don't want to have any connection.

TOMMY. You needn't say no more—a nod's as good as a wink to a blind horse—you've no meddlin' or makin' with it good, bad, or indifferent, pro nor con ; I knew it an' Minnie knows it—give me your hand. (*He catches* DAVOREN's *hand.*) Two firm hands clasped together will all the power outbrave of the heartless English tyrant, the Saxon coward an' knave. That's Tommy Owens' hand, Mr. Davoren, the hand of a man, a man—Mr. Shields knows me well. (*He breaks into song to the air:* " Tramp, tramp, tramp.")

High upon the gallows tree stood the noble-hearted three,
By the vengeful tyrant stricken in their bloom;
But they met him face to face with the spirit of their race,
And they went with souls undaunted to their doom!

MINNIE (*loudly, in an effort to quell his fervour*).   Tommy Owens'
for goodness' sake . . .

TOMMY (*overwhelming her with a shout*).   God save Ireland ses the
hayros, God save Ireland ses we all
Whether on the scaffold high or the battlefield we die,
Oh, what matter when for Ayryinn dear we fall!

(OWENS *ends the song and stands for a moment sadly.   Then he turns
plaintively towards* DAVOREN.)

TOMMY (*tearfully*).   Mr. Davoren, I'd die for Ireland!

(DAVOREN *goes, in front of table, to* OWENS *and pats him on the
shoulder.*)

DAVOREN.   I know you would, I know you would, Tommy.

TOMMY.   I never got a chance—they never gave me a chance
—but all the same I'd be there if I was called on—Mr. Shields
knows that—ask Mr. Shields, Mr. Davoren.

DAVOREN.   There's no necessity, Tommy; I know you're the
right stuff if you got the chance, but remember that " he also serves
who only stands and waits."   (*He goes back to his place behind table.*)

TOMMY (*fiercely*).   I'm bloody well tired o' waitin'—we're all
tired o' waitin'.   Why isn't every man in Ireland out with the
I.R.A. ?   Up with the barricades, up with the barricades; it's
now or never, now an' for ever, as Sarsfield said at the battle o'
Vinegar Hill.   Up with the barricades—that's Tommy Owens—
an' a penny buys a whistle.   Let them as thinks different say
different—what do you say, Mr. Davoren ?

DAVOREN.   I say, Tommy, you ought to go up and get your
dinner, for if you wait much longer it won't be worth eating.

TOMMY.   Oh, damn the dinner; who'd think o' dinner an' Ireland
fightin' to be free—not Tommy Owens, anyhow.   It's only the
Englishman who's always thinkin' of his belly.

MINNIE.   Tommy Owens!

TOMMY.   Excuse me, Miss Powell, in the ardure ov me anger I
disremembered there was a lady present.

(*Voices are heard outside, and presently* MRS. HENDERSON *comes into
the room, followed by* MR. GALLOPHER, *who, however, lingers at the
door, too timid to come any farther.   MRS. HENDERSON is a massive
woman in every way; massive head, arms and body; massive
voice, and a massive amount of self-confidence.   She is a mountain
of good nature, and during the interview she behaves towards* DAVOREN
*with deferential self-assurance.   She dominates the room, and seems
to occupy the whole of it.   She is dressed poorly, but tidily, wearing*

a white apron and a large shawl. MR. GALLOPHER, *on the other hand, is a spare little man with a spare little grey beard, and a thin, nervous voice. He is dressed as well as a faded suit of blue will allow him to be. He stands half in and half out of the door,* R. *He is obviously ill at ease during his interview with* DAVOREN. *He carries a hard hat, much the worse for wear, under his left arm, and a letter in his right hand.*)

MRS. HENDERSON (*looking back at* GALLOGHER, *entering the room* R.). Come along in, Mr. Gallicker, Mr. Davoren won't mind ; it's him as can put you in the way o' havin' your wrongs righted ; come on in, man, an' don't be so shy—Mr. Davoren is wan ov ourselves that stands for govermint ov the people with the people by the people. You'll find you'll be as welcome as the flowers in May. (*To* DAVOREN.) Good evenin', Mr. Davoren, an' God an' His holy angels be between you an' all harm.

TOMMY (*effusively*). Come on, Mr. Gallicker, an' don't be a stranger—we're all friends here—anything special to be done or particular advice asked, here's your man here.

DAVOREN (*subconsciously pleased, but a little timid of the belief that he is connected with the gunmen*). I'm very busy just now, Mrs. Henderson, and really . . .

MRS. HENDERSON (*mistaking the reason of his embarrassment*). Don't be put out, Mr. Davoren, we won't keep you more nor a few minutes. It's not in me or in Mr. Gallicker to spoil sport. Him an' me was young once, an' knows what it is to be sthrollin at night in the pale moonlight, with arms round one another. (*Turning to look at* GALLOGHER *with a grin on her face.*) An' I wouldn't take much an' say there's game in Mr. Gallicker still, for I seen, sometimes, a dangerous cock in his eye. (*Turning to* DAVOREN.) But we won't keep you an' Minnie long asunder ; he's the letther an' all written. You must know Mr. Davoren—excuse me for not inthroducin' him sooner. (*Looking at* DAVOREN *and extending her hand towards* MR. GALLOGHER.) This is Mr. Gallicker—(GALLOGHER *bows deeply*)—who lives in the front drawing-room of number fifty-five ; as decent an' honest an' quiet a man as you'd never meet in a day's walk. An' signs on it, it's them as'll be imposed upon—read the letther, Mr. Gallicker.

(GALLOGHER *crosses front of* MRS. HENDERSON, *and stands* R. *side of table, upstage.* MINNIE *goes to fireplace.* OWENS *goes a little behind* GALLOGHER, *to look over his shoulder.* MRS. HENDERSON *stands* L.R.C. DAVOREN *stands* L. *side of table, downstage.*)

TOMMY. Read away, Mr. Gallicker, it will be attended to, never fear ; we know our own know, eh, Mr. Davoren ?

MINNIE (*impatiently*). Hurry up, Mr. Gallicker, an' don't be keeping Mr. Davoren.

MRS. HENDERSON. Give him time, Minnie Powell. Give him

time. You must know in all fairity, Mr. Davoren, that the family livin' in the next room to Mr. Gallicker—the back drawin'-room, to be particular—am I right or am I wrong, Mr. Gallicker ?

MR. GALLOGHER. You're right, Mrs. Henderson, perfectly right, indeed—that's the very identical room.

MRS. HENDERSON. Well, Mr. Davoren, the people in the back drawing-room ought to be more particular, the residents that's the word that's writ in the letter—(*turning to* GALLOGHER)—am I right or am I wrong, Mr. Gallogher ?

GALLOGHER (*peering into letter*). You're right, Mrs. Henderson, perfectly accurate—that's the very identical word.

MRS. HENDERSON (*to* DAVOREN). Well, Mr. Davoren, the residents in the back drawin'-room, as I aforesaid, is nothin' but a gang o' tramps that oughtn't to be allowed to associate with honest, decent, quiet, respectable people. Mr. Gallicker has tried to reason with them, and make them behave themselves—which in my opinion they never will—however, that's only an opinion, an' not legal— ever since they have made Mr. Gallicker's life a HELL ! Mr. Gallicker, am I right or am I wrong ?

MR. GALLOGHER. I'm sorry to say you're right, Mrs. Henderson, perfectly right—not a word of exaggeration.

MRS. HENDERSON. Well, now, Mr. Gallicker, seein' as I have given Mr. Davoren a fair account of how you're situated, an' of these tramps' cleverality, I'll ask you to read the letter, which I'll say, not because you're there, or that you're a friend o' mine, is as good a letter as was decomposed by a scholar. Now, Mr. Gallicker, an' don't forget the top sayin'.

(MR. GALLOGHER *prepares to read, arranges his spectacles on nose.* TOMMY *takes out a well-worn notebook and a pencil stump, and assumes a very important attitude.*)

TOMMY (*stopping* GALLOGHER). One second. Mr. Gallicker, is this the twenty-first or twenty-second ?

MR. GALLOGHER. The twenty-first, sir.

TOMMY. Thanks ; proceed, Mr. Gallicker.

MR. GALLOGHER (*with a few preliminary tremors, begins to read. Reading*) :

> " To ALL to WHOM THESE PRESENTS COME,
> GREETING
> Gentlemen of the Irish Republican Army."

MRS. HENDERSON (*interrupting*). There's a beginnin' for you, Mr. Davoren.

MINNIE. That's some swank.

TOMMY. There's a lot in that sayin', mind you ; it's a hard wallop at the British Empire.

MRS. HENDERSON (*proudly*). Go on, Mr. Gallicker.

MR. GALLOGHER (*reading*) :

" I wish to call your attention to the persecution me and my family has to put up with in respect of and appertaining to the residents of the back drawing-room of the house known as fifty-five, Saint Teresa Street, situate in the Parish of St. Thomas, in the Borough and City of Dublin. This persecution started eighteen months ago—or to be precise—on the tenth day of the sixth month, in the year nineteen hundred and twenty."

MRS. HENDERSON (*interrupting*). That's the word I was trying to think ov—precise—it cuts the ground from under their feet—so to speak.

MR. GALLOGHER (*reading*) :

" We, the complainants, resident on the ground floor, deeming it disrespectable . . ."

MRS. HENDERSON (*with an emphatic nod*). Which it was.

MR. GALLOGHER (*reading*) :

" Deeming it disrespectable to have an open hall door, and to have the hall turned into a playground, made a solemn protest, and, in consequence, we the complainants aforesaid has had no peace ever since. Owing to the persecution, as aforesaid specified, we had to take out a summons again them some time ago as there was no Republican Courts then ; but we did not proceed again them as me and my wife—to wit, James and Winifred Gallogher—has a strong objection to foreign Courts as such. We had peace for some time after that, but now things have gone from bad to worse. The name calling and the language is something abominable. . . ."

MRS. HENDERSON (*holding out her hand as a constable would extend his to stop a car that another may pass*). Excuse me, Mr. Gallicker, but I think the word " shockin' " should be put in there after abominable ; for the language used be these tramps has two ways o' bein' looked at—for it's abominable to the childer an' shockin' to your wife—am I right or am I wrong, Mr. Davoren ?

TOMMY (*judicially*). Shockin' is a right good word, with a great deal o' meanin', an' . . .

MRS. HENDERSON (*with a deprecating gesture that extinguishes* TOMMY). Tommy, let Mr. Davoren speak ; whatever Mr. Davoren ses, Julia Henderson'll abide be.

DAVOREN (*afraid to say anything else*). I think the word might certainly be introduced with advantage.

MRS. HENDERSON. Go over there, Mr. Gallicker, an' put in the word shockin', as aforesaid.

(GALLOGHER *goes over to the table, gets pen, and with a great deal of difficulty enters the word.*)

TOMMY (*to* MR. GALLOGHER *as he writes*). Ey, there's two k's in shockin' !

MR. GALLOGHER (*gives a withering look of scorn at* OWENS, *and goes on reading*) :

"The language is something abominable and shocking. My wife has often to lock the door of the room to keep them from assaulting her. The name of the resident-tenant who is giving all this trouble and who, pursuant to the facts of the case aforesaid, mentioned, will be the defendant, is Dwyer. The husband of the aforesaid Mrs. Dwyer, or the aforesaid defendant, as the case may be, is a seaman, who is coming home shortly, and we beg The Irish Republican Army to note that the said Mrs. Dwyer says he will settle us when he comes home. While leaving it entirely in the hands of the gentlemen of The Republican Army, the defendant, that is to say, James Gallogher of fifty-five St. Teresa Street, ventures to say that he thinks he has made out a Primmy Fashy Case against Mrs. Dwyer and all her heirs, male and female as aforesaid mentioned in the above written schedule.

"N.B.—If you send up any of your men, please tell them to bring their guns. I beg to remain the humble servant and devoted admirer of the Gentlemen of the Irish Republican Army.

"Witness my hand this tenth day of the fifth month of the year nineteen hundred and twenty.

"JAMES GALLOGHER."

(*Taking off spectacles, with a modest cough*). Ahem.

MRS. HENDERSON (*proudly, to* DAVOREN). There's a letter for you, Mr. Davoren !

TOMMY (*fervently*). It's the most powerfullest letter I ever heard read.

MINNIE. It wasn't you, really, that writ it, Mr. Gallicker ?

MRS. HENDERSON (*to* MINNIE). Sinn Fein Amhain : him an' him only, Minnie. I seen him with me own two eyes when me an' Winnie—Mrs. Gallicker, Mr. Davoren, aforesaid as appears in the letter—was havin' a chat be the fire.

MINNIE. You'd never think it was in him to do it.

MRS. HENDERSON. An' to think that the likes ov such a man is to have the sowl-case worried out ov him by a gang o' tramps ; but it's in good hands now, an' instead ov them settlin' yous, Mr. Gallicker, it's yous 'ill settle them. Give the letter to Mr. Davoren, an' we'll be goin'.

(GALLOGHER *comes from* C. *to table and hands the letter to* DAVOREN, *who takes it and puts it on the table.* GALLOGHER *then crosses front of* OWENS *and* MRS. HENDERSON, *to* R. MRS. HENDERSON *follows him a step, then turns a little towards* DAVOREN.)

(*To* DAVOREN.) I hope you an' Mr. Shields is gettin' on all right together, Mr. Davoren.

DAVOREN. Fairly well, thanks, Mrs. Henderson. We don't see much of each other. He's out during the day, and I'm usually out during the evening.

MRS. HENDERSON. I'm afraid he'll never make a fortune out

ov what he's sellin'. He'll talk above an hour over a pennorth o' pins. Every time he comes to our place I buy a package o' hairpins from him to give him a little encouragement. I 'clare to God I have as many pins now as ud make a wire mattress for a double bed. All the young divils about the place are beginnin' to make a jeer ov him, too ; I gave one ov them a mallavogin' the other day for callin' him oul' hairpins !

MR. GALLOGHER (*venturing an opinion turning to face the others*). Mr. Shields is a man of exceptional mental capacity, and is worthy of a more dignified position.

MRS. HENDERSON. Them words is true, Mr. Gallicker, and they aren't. For to be wise is to be a fool, an' to be a fool is to be wise.

MR. GALLOGHER (*with deprecating tolerance*). Oh, Mrs. Henderson, that's a parrotox.

MRS. HENDERSON. It may be what a parrot talks, or a blackbird, or, for the matter of that, a lark—but it's what Julia Henderson thinks, any . . . whisht, is that a *Stop Press* ?

(*Outside is heard the shriek of a newsboy calling " Stop Press." They all listen.*)

Run out, Tommy, an' get it till we see what it is.

TOMMY. I haven't got a make.

MRS. HENDERSON (*crossly*). I never seen you any other way, an' you'll be always the same if you keep follyin' your Spearmints, an' your Bumble Bees an' your Night Patrols. (*Opening door* R. *and shouting to someone outside.*) Is that a *Stop Press*, Mrs. Grigson ?

VOICE (*outside door* R.). Yis ; an ambush out near Knocksedan.

MRS. HENDERSON. That's the stuff to give them. (*Loudly.*) Was there anybody hurted ?

VOICE (*outside*). One poor man killed—some chap named Maguire, the paper says.

DAVOREN (*agitated*). What name did she say ?

MINNIE (*to* DAVOREN, *noticing his agitation*). Maguire ; did you know him, Mr. Davoren ?

DAVOREN. Yes—no, no ; I didn't know him, no, I didn't know him, Minnie.

MINNIE. I wonder is it the Maguire that does be with Mr. Shields ?

DAVOREN. Oh no, not at all, it couldn't be.

MRS. HENDERSON (*to* GALLOGHER). Well, I think we'd betther make a move, Mr. Gallicker ; we've kep' Mr. Davoren long enough, an' you'll find the letther'll be in good hands.

(GALLOGHER, *near door* R., *suddenly turns, and, crossing in front of* MRS. HENDERSON, *ambles over to* R. *side of table, buttoning his coat nervously as he does so, and speaks formally and respectfully to* DAVOREN.)

GALLOGHER. Mr. Davoren, sir, on behalf ov meself, James

Gallicker, an' Winifred, Mrs. Gallicker, wife ov the said James, I beg to offer, extend an' furnish our humble an' hearty thanks for your benevolent goodness in interferin' in the matter specified, particularated an' expanded upon in the letter, mandamus or schedule, as the case may be. An' let me interpretate to you on behalf ov meself an' Winifred Gallicker, that whenever you visit us you will be supernally positive of a hundred thousand welcomes—ahem.

MRS. HENDERSON (*to* DAVOREN, *beaming with pride for the genius of her friend*). There's a man for you, Mr. Davoren ! He forgot to mention Biddy and Shaun, his two children—it's himself has them trained well. It ud make your heart thrill like an alarm clock to hear them singin' " Faith ov Our Fathers " an' " Wrap the Green Flag Roun' Me."

MR. GALLOGHER (*half-apologetically and half-proudly*). Faith an' Fatherland, Mrs. Henderson, Faith and Fatherland. (*Crosses front of* MRS. HENDERSON *to door,* R.)

MRS. HENDERSON. Well, good day, Mr. Davoren, an' God keep you an' strengthen all the men that are fightin' for Ireland's freedom.

(*She and* GALLOGHER *go out door,* R.)

TOMMY. I must be off too, so long, Mr. Davoren, an' remember that Tommy Owens only waits the call.

(*He goes out to door,* R.)

(DAVOREN *watches them go, then turns from* L. *of table, and joins* MINNIE *at fireplace, and puts an arm around her.*)

DAVOREN (*delighted*). Well, Minnie, we're by ourselves once more.

MINNIE. Wouldn't that Tommie Owens give you the sick ! Only waitin' to hear the call ! Ah, then it ud take all the brass bands in the country to blow the call, before Tommie Owens ud hear it. (*She looks at wristlet watch.*) Sacred Heart, I've only ten minutes to get back to work—I'll have to fly ! (*She moves to table.*) Quick, Mr. Davoren, write me name in typewritin' before I go—just " Minnie."

(DAVOREN *comes down to table, sits at typewriter, and rapidly types the name.*)

(*Shyly.*) Now yours underneath—just " Donal."

(DAVOREN *rapidly does so.*)

(MINNIE *takes the paper from the typewriter, and reads the names.*)

(*Reading.*) Minnie, Donal ; Donal, Minnie.

(*She folds them up and puts the paper down the front of her blouse.*)

(*To* DAVOREN). Good-bye now.

(MINNIE *is running towards the door,* R., *when* DONAL *calls her back with a question.*)

DAVOREN.   Here, what about your milk ?
MINNIE.   I haven't time to take it now.   (*Slyly*) I'll come for it this evening.

(*They both go towards the door,* R.)

DAVOREN.   Minnie, the kiss I didn't get.
MINNIE.   What kiss ?
DAVOREN.   When we were interrupted ; you know, you little rogue, come, just one.
MINNIE.   Quick, then.

(DAVOREN *kisses her and she runs out door,* R.   DAVOREN *returns thoughtfully to the table and stands behind it.*)

DAVOREN.   Minnie, Donal ; Donal, Minnie.   Very pretty, but very ignorant.   A Gunman on the run !   Be careful, be careful, Donal Davoren.   But Minnie is attracted to the idea, and I am attracted to Minnie.   And what danger can there be in being the shadow of a gunman ?

CURTAIN.

ACT II

SCENE.—*The same as in Act I. But it is now night.* SEUMAS *is in the bed that runs along the wall at back.* DAVOREN *is seated at the table. He has a fountain-pen in his hand, and is attracted in thought towards the moon, which is shining in through the windows. An open writing-pad is on the table at* DAVOREN'S *elbow. The bag left by* MAGUIRE *is still under the bed,* R., *a lighted candle is on the table beside the typewriter.*

DAVOREN. The cold chaste moon, the Queen of Heaven's bright isles,

> Who makes all beautiful on which she smiles;
> That wandering shrine of soft yet icy flame,
> Which ever is transformed yet still the same.

Ah, Shelley, Shelley, you yourself were a lovely human orb shining through clouds of whirling human dust. " She makes all beautiful on which she smiles." Ah, Shelley, she couldn't make this accursed room beautiful. Donal, Donal, I fear your last state is worse than your first.

(He lilts a verse, which he writes in the pad before him.)

> When night advances through the sky with slow
>   And solemn tread,
> The queenly moon looks down on life below,
>   As if she read
> Man's soul, and in her scornful silence said:
>   All beautiful and happiest things are dead.

SEUMAS (*sleepily, lying flat on his back*). Donal, Donal, are you awake? (*A pause.*) Donal, Donal, are you asleep?

DAVOREN. I'm neither awake nor asleep: I'm thinking.

SEUMAS. I was just thinkin', too—I was just thinkin', too, that Maguire is sorry now that he didn't come with me instead of going to Knocksedan. He caught something besides butterflies—two of them he got, one through each lung.

DAVOREN. The Irish people are very fond of turning a serious thing into a joke; that was a serious affair—for poor Maguire.

SEUMAS (*defensively*). Why didn't he do what he arranged to do? Did he think of me when he was goin' to Knocksedan? How can he expect me to have any sympathy with him now?

26

DAVOREN. He can hardly expect that now that he's dead.

SEUMAS. The Republicans 'll do a lot for him, now. How am I goin' to get back the things he has belongin' to me, either ? There's some of them in that bag under the bed here, but that's not quarter of what he had ; an' I don't know where he was stoppin', for he left his old digs a week or so ago—I suppose there's nothing to be said about my loss ; I'm to sing dumb.

DAVOREN (*suddenly looking over at* SEUMAS). I hope there's nothing else in the bag, besides thread and hairpins.

SEUMAS. What else ud be in it ? . . . I can't sleep properly ever since they put on this damned curfew. A minute ago I thought I heard some of the oul' ones standin' at the door ; they won't be satisfied till they bring a raid on the house ; an' they never begin to stand at the door till after curfew. . . . Are you gone to bed, Donal ?

DAVOREN. No ; I'm trying to finish this poem.

SEUMAS (*turning over on side to look at* DAVOREN). If I was you I'd give that game up ; it doesn't pay a working man to write poetry. I don't profess to know much about poetry—I don't profess to know much about poetry—about poetry—I don't know much about the pearly glint of the morning dew, or the damask sweetness of the rare wild rose, or the subtle greenness of the serpent's eye—but I think a poet's claim to greatness depends upon his power to put passion in the common people.

DAVOREN. Ay, passion to howl for his destruction. The People ! Damn the people ! They live in the abyss, the poet lives on the mountain-top ; to the people there is no mystery of colour : it is simply the scarlet coat of the soldier ; the purple vestments of a priest ; the green banner of a party ; the brown or blue overalls of industry. The people——

(SEUMAS *suddenly sits up in bed, resting on his elbow, listening intently*.)

(*With a deep note of anxiety in his voice*). Whisht, is that the tapping again ?

DAVOREN (*startled into interest by the evident anxiety of* SEUMAS). Tappin' ? What tappin' ?

SEUMAS (*in an awed whisper*). This is the second night I heard that tappin' ! I believe it bodes no good to me. There, do you hear it again—a quiet, steady, mysterious tappin' on the wall.

DAVOREN (*listening intently*). I hear no tappin'.

SEUMAS (*lying down again, anxious*). It ud be better for me if you did. It's a sure sign of death when nobody hears it but meself.

DAVOREN. Death ! What the devil are you talking about, man ?

SEUMAS. I don't like it at all ; there's always something like that heard when one of our family dies.

DAVOREN. I don't know about that ; but I know there's a hell of a lot of things heard when one of your family lives.

SEUMAS. God between us an' all harm ! Thank God I'm where

I ought to be—in bed. It's always best to be in your proper place when such things happen. (*He springs up in bed again, in great fear.*) Sacred Heart, there it is again ! (*Turns to look at* DAVOREN.) Do you not hear it now ?

DAVOREN (*losing patience*). Aw, for God's sake, go asleep !

SEUMAS (*vehemently*). Do you believe in nothin' ?

DAVOREN (*scornfully*). I don't believe in tappin'.

SEUMAS (*listening intently*). Whisht, it's stopped now. (*He stretches himself down again.*) I'll try to go to sleep for fear it ud begin again.

DAVOREN (*resuming work*). Ay do ; and if it does, I'll be sure to waken you up.

(*A longer pause than usual, during which* SEUMAS *gives a few restless movements in bed.*)

SEUMAS (*with a restless movement in bed*). It's very cold to-night —do you feel cold ?

DAVOREN (*with an angry appeal*). I thought you were goin' asleep ?

SEUMAS. The bloody cold won't let me. . . . You'd want a pair of pyjamas on you. (*A pause.*) Did you ever wear pyjamas, Donal ?

DAVOREN. No, no, no.

SEUMAS. What kind of stuff is in them ?

DAVOREN (*angrily*). Oh, it depends on the climate ; in India, silk ; in Italy, satin ; and the Eskimo wears them made from the skin of the Polar bear.

SEUMAS (*emphatically*). If you take my advice you'll get into bed—that poem is beginnin' to get on your nerves.

(DAVOREN *viciously blows out the candle on table, moves to* R. *side of bed,* L., *and, beginning to undress, takes off his coat.*)

DAVOREN (R. *of bed,* L.). Right ; I'm goin' to bed now, so you can shut up.

(*A little longer pause ;* SEUMAS *stretched on back in bed ;* DAVOREN *with a surly look on his face, undressing. He just takes off coat and vest, and then sits on side of bed moodily.*)

SEUMAS. I was goin' to say something when you put out the light —what's this it was—um, um, oh, ay : when I was comin' in this evenin' I saw Minnie Powell goin' out. If I was you I wouldn't have that one comin' in here.

DAVOREN. She comes in ; I don't bring her in, do I ?

SEUMAS. The oul' ones'll be talkin', an' once they start you don't know how it'll end. Surely a man that has read Shelley couldn't be interested in an ignorant little bitch that thinks of nothin' but jazz dances, fox trots, picture theatres an' dress.

DAVOREN. Right glad I am that she thinks of dress, for she

thinks of it in the right way, and makes herself a pleasant picture to the eye. Education has been wasted on many persons, teaching them to talk only, but leaving with them all their primitive instincts. Had poor Minnie received an education she would have been an artist. She is certainly a pretty girl. I'm sure she is a good girl, and I believe she is a brave girl.

Seumas. A Helen of Troy come to live in a tenement ! You think a lot about her simply because she thinks a lot about you, an' she thinks a lot about you because she looks upon you as a hero —a kind o' Paris . . . she'd give the world an' all to be gaddin' about with a gunman. An' what ecstasy it ud give her if after a bit you were shot or hanged ; she'd be able to go about then—like a good many more—singin', "I do not mourn me darlin' lost, for he fell in his Jacket Green." An' then, for a year an' a day, all round her hat she'd wear the Tri-coloured Ribbon O, till she'd pick up an' marry someone else—possibly a British Tommy, with a Mons Star. An' as for bein' brave, it's easy to be that when you've no cause for cowardice ; I wouldn't care to have me life dependin' on brave little Minnie Powell—(*turning viciously on his side, so that his back is to audience*) she wouldn't sacrifice a jazz dance to save it.

Davoren (*sitting on the bed and taking off his coat and vest, preparatory to going to bed*). There ; that's enough about Minnie Powell. I'm afraid I'll soon have to be on the run out of this house, too ; it is becoming painfully obvious that there is no peace to be found here.

Seumas. Oh, this house is all right ; barrin' the children, it does be quiet enough. Wasn't there children in the last place you were in, too ?

Davoren. Ay, ten ; (*viciously*) and they were all over forty.

(*A pause as* Davoren *is removing his collar and tie.*)

Seumas (*turning on to his back*). Everything is very quiet now ; I wonder what time is it ?

Davoren. The village cock hath thrice done salutation to the morn.

Seumas. Shakespeare, Richard the Third, Act Five, Scene III. It was Ratcliffe said that to Richard just before the battle of Bosworth. . . . How peaceful the heavens look now with the moon in the middle ; you'd never think there were men prowlin' about tryin' to shoot each other. I don't know how a man who has shot anyone can sleep in peace at night.

Davoren. There's plenty of men can't sleep in peace at night now unless they know that they have shot somebody.

Seumas. I wish to God it was all over. The country is gone mad. Instead of counting their beads now they're countin' bullets ; their Hail Marys and paternosters are burstin' bombs—burstin' bombs, an' the rattle of machine guns ; petrol is their holy water ; their Mass is a burnin' buildin' ; their De Profundis is " The Soldiers'

Song," an' their creed is, I believe in the gun almighty, maker of
heaven an' earth—an' it's all for " the glory o' God an' the honour
o' Ireland."

DAVOREN. I remember the time when you yourself believed in
nothing but the gun.

SEUMAS (*quickly*). Ay, when there wasn't a gun in the country ;
I've a different opinion now when there's nothin' but guns in the
country. . . . An' you daren't open your mouth, for Kathleen
Ni Houlihan is very different now to the woman who used to play
the harp an' sing " Weep on, weep on, your hour is past," for she's a
ragin' divil now, an' if you only look crooked at her you're sure of
a punch in th' eye. (*On elbow in bed, eagerly to* DAVOREN.) But
this is the way I look at it—I look at it this way : You're not goin'
—you're not goin' to beat the British Empire—the British Empire,
by shootin' an occasional Tommy at the corner of an occasional
street. Besides, when the Tommies have the wind up—when the
Tommies have the wind up they let bang at everything they see—
they don't give a God's curse who they plug.

DAVOREN (*ironically ; looking over at* SEUMAS). Maybe they ought
to get down off the lorry and run to the Records Office to find out a
man's pedigree before they plug him.

SEUMAS. It's the civilians that suffer ; when there's an ambush
they don't know where to run. Shot in the back to save the British
Empire, an' shot in the breast to save the soul of Ireland. I'm a
Nationalist meself, right enough—a Nationalist right enough, but
all the same—I'm a Nationalist right enough ; I believe in the freedom of Ireland, an' that England has no right to be here, but I draw
the line when I hear the gunmen blowin' about dyin' for the people,
when it's the people that are dyin' for the gunmen ! With all due
respect to the gunmen, I don't want them to die for me.

DAVOREN (*jeeringly*). Not likely ; you object to any one of
them deliberately dying for you for fear that one of these days you
might accidentally die for one of them.

SEUMAS (*ironically*). You're one of the brave fellows that doesn't
fear death.

DAVOREN (*conceitedly*). Why should I be afraid of it ? It's all
the same to me how it comes, where it comes or when it comes. I
leave fear of death to the people that are always praying for eternal
life ; (*philosophically*) " Death is here and death is there, death is
busy everywhere."

SEUMAS. Ay, in Ireland. Thanks be to God I'm a daily com-
municant. There's a great comfort in religion ; it makes a man
strong in time of trouble an' brave in time of danger. No man need
be afraid with a crowd of angels round him ; thanks to God for His
Holy religion !

DAVOREN. You're welcome to your angels ; philosophy is mine ;
philosophy that makes the coward brave ; the sufferer defiant ; the
weak strong ; the . . .

(*A shot rings out in the lane outside window,* C., *back, and religion and philosophy are forgotten.* DAVOREN *crouches down on floor, near bed,* L. SEUMAS *flattens himself in bed, and almost covers his face with the clothes. The next few sentences are spoken rapidly and in fear.*)

SEUMAS (*rapidly*).   Jesus, Mary an' Joseph, what's that ?

DAVOREN (*rapidly*).   My God, that's very close.

SEUMAS.   Is there no Christianity at all left in the country ?

DAVOREN (*rapidly*).   Are we ever again going to know what peace and security are ?

SEUMAS (*rapidly*).   If this continues much longer I'll be nothing but a galvanic battery o' shocks.

DAVOREN (*rapidly*).   It's dangerous to be in and it's equally dangerous to be out.

SEUMAS (*after a moment's thought*).   This is a dangerous spot to be in with that window ; you couldn't tell the minute a bullet ud come in through it—through it, an' hit the—hit the—an' hit the . . .

DAVOREN (*with nervous intensity*).   Hit the what, man ?

SEUMAS.   The wall !

DAVOREN (*sitting on side of bed,* L.).   Couldn't you say that at first without making a song about it.

SEUMAS (*suddenly, after a pause*).   I don't believe there's horses in the stable at all.

DAVOREN (*mystified*).   Stable !   What stable are you talking about ?

SEUMAS.   There's a stable at the back of the house with an entrance from the yard ; it's used as a carpenter's shop.   Didn't you often hear the peculiar noises at night ?   They give out that it's the horses shakin' their chains.

(DAVOREN *comes over to bed* SEUMAS *is in, stands at the head, bends down towards* SEUMAS, *nervously interested in what* SEUMAS *has said.*)

DAVOREN (*with concern*).   An' what is it ?

SEUMAS.   Oh, there I'll leave you !

DAVOREN.   Surely you don't mean . . .

SEUMAS.   But I do mean it.

DAVOREN.   You do mean what ?

SEUMAS.   I wouldn't—I wouldn't be surprised—wouldn't be surprised—surprised.

DAVOREN (*impatient*).   Yes, yes, surprised—go on.

SEUMAS.   I wouldn't be surprised if they were manufacturin' bombs there.

DAVOREN (*horrified*).   My God, that's a pleasant contemplation ! The sooner I'm on the run out of this house the better.   How is it you never said anything about this before ?

SEUMAS (*hesitant*).   Well—well, I didn't want—I didn't want to —to . . .

DAVOREN. You didn't want to what ?

SEUMAS. I didn't want to frighten you.

DAVOREN (*sarcastically goes back to side of bed,* L.). You're bloody kind !

(*A knock at the door ; the voice of* MRS. GRIGSON *heard.*)

MRS. GRIGSON. Are you asleep, Mr. Shields ?

SEUMAS (*with intense annoyance*). What the devil can she want at this hour of the night ? (*To* MRS. GRIGSON.) No, Mrs. Grigson, what is it ?

MRS. GRIGSON (*opening the door and standing just inside the threshold. She is a woman about* 40, *but looks much older. She is one of the cave-dwellers of Dublin, living as she does in a tenement kitchen, to which only an occasional sickly beam of sunlight filters through a grating in the yard ; the consequent general dimness of her abode has given her a habit of peering through half-closed eyes. She is slovenly dressed in an old skirt and bodice ; her face is grimy, not because her habits are dirty—for, although she is untidy, she is a clean woman— but because of the smoky atmosphere of her room. Her hair is constantly falling over her face, which she is as frequently removing by rapid movements of her right hand*). He hasn't turned up yet, an' I'm stiff with the cold waitin' for him.

SEUMAS. Mr. Grigson, is it ?

MRS. GRIGSON (*looking over at* SEUMAS). Adolphus, Mr. Shields, after takin' his tea at six o'clock—no, I'm tellin' a lie—it was before six, for I remember the Angelus was ringin' out an' we sittin' at the table—after takin' his tea he went out for a breath o' fresh air, an' I haven't seen sign or light of him since. 'Clare to God me heart is up in me mouth, thinkin' he might be shot be the Black an' Tans.

SEUMAS. Aw, he'll be all right, Mrs. Grigson. You ought to go to bed an' rest yourself ; it's always the worst that comes into a body's mind ; go to bed, Mrs. Grigson, or you'll catch your death of cold.

MRS. GRIGSON. I'm afraid to go to bed, Mr. Shields, for I'm always in dread that some night or another, when he has a sup taken, he'll fall down the kitchen stairs an' break his neck. Not that I'd be any the worse if anything did happen to him, for you know the sort he is, Mr. Shields ; sure he has me heart broke.

SEUMAS. Don't be downhearted, Mrs. Grigson ; he may take a thought one of these days an' turn over a new leaf.

MRS. GRIGSON. Sorra leaf Adolphus 'll ever turn over, he's too far gone in the horns for that now. Sure no one ud mind him takin' a pint or two, if he'd stop at that, but he won't ; nothin' could fill him with beer, an' no matter how much he may have taken, when he's taken more he'll always say, " here's the first to-day."

(*She goes to door,* R., *opens it, and looks out.*)

DAVOREN (*to* SEUMAS). Christ! Is she going to stop talking there all the night?

SEUMAS (*warningly*). 'Sh, she'll hear you; right enough, the man has the poor woman's heart broke.

DAVOREN. And because he has her heart broken, she's to have the privilege of breaking everybody else's.

MRS. GRIGSON (*coming back, and over to* SEUMAS). Mr. Shields.

SEUMAS. Yes?

MRS. GRIGSON. Do the insurance companies pay if a man is shot after curfew?

SEUMAS. Well, now, that's a thing I couldn't say, Mrs. Grigson.

MRS. GRIGSON (*plaintively*). Isn't he a terrible man to be takin' such risks, an' not knowin' what'll happen to him. He knows them. Societies only want an excuse to do people out of their money—is it after one, now, Mr. Shields?

SEUMAS. Aw, it must be after one, Mrs. Grigson.

MRS. GRIGSON (*emphatically*). Ah, then, if I was a young girl again I'd think twice before gettin' married. Whisht! There's somebody now—it's him, I know be the way he's fumblin'.

(*She goes out a little way, by door,* R. *Stumbling steps are heard outside.*)

(*Outside*). Is that you, Dolphie, dear?

(*After a few moments,* ADOLPHUS, *with* MRS. GRIGSON *holding his arm, stumbles into the room.*)

(R.) Dolphie, dear, mind yourself.

ADOLPHUS (L. *of* MRS. GRIGSON. *He is a man of 55, but looks, relatively, much younger than* MRS. GRIGSON. *His occupation is that of a solicitor's clerk. He has all the appearance of being well fed; and, in fact, he gets most of the nourishment,* MRS. GRIGSON *getting just enough to give her strength to do the necessary work of the household. On account of living most of his life out of the kitchen, his complexion is fresh, and his movements, even when sober, are livelier than those of his wife. He is comfortably dressed; heavy top-coat, soft trilby hat, a fancy-coloured scarf about his neck, and he carries an umbrella*). I'm all right; do you see anything wrong with me?

MRS. GRIGSON. Of course you're all right, dear; there's no one mindin' you.

ADOLPHUS GRIGSON (*scornfully*). Mindin' me, is it, mindin' me? He'd want to be a good thing that ud mind me. There's a man here—a man, mind you, afraid av nothin'—not in this bloody house anyway.

MRS. GRIGSON (*imploringly*). Come on downstairs, Dolphie, dear; sure there's not one in the house ud say a word to you.

ADOLPHUS GRIGSON (*with strong emphasis*). Say a word to me, is it? He'd want to be a good thing that ud say anything to Dolphus Grigson. (*Loudly.*) Is there anyone wants to say anything

to Dolphus Grigson ? If there is, he's here—a man, too—there's
no blottin' it out—a man.

MRS. GRIGSON.   You'll wake everybody in the house ; can't you
speak quiet.

ADOLPHUS GRIGSON (*more loudly still*).   What do I care for anybody in the house ? Are they keepin' me ; are they givin' me
anthing ? When they're keepin' Grigson it'll be time enough for
them to talk. (*With a shout.*)   I can tell them Adolphus Grigson
wasn't born in a bottle !

MRS. GRIGSON (*tearfully*).   Why do you talk like that, dear ; we
all know you weren't born in a bottle.

ADOLPHUS GRIGSON.   There's some of them in this house think
that Grigson was born in a bottle.

DAVOREN (*with conviction, to* SEUMAS).   A most appropriate place
for him to be born in.

MRS. GRIGSON (*to* MR. GRIGSON *while trying to lead him out by
door,* R.).   Come on down to bed, an' you can talk about them in
the mornin'.

ADOLPHUS GRIGSON (*breaking* MRS. GRIGSON'S *hold on his arm as he
reaches door,* R. *and moving unsteadily farther* L.).   I'll talk about
them now.   D'ye think I'm afraid of them ? (*With conceited conviction.*)   Adolphus Grigson's afraid av nothin', creepin' or walkin'
—(*he stands upright and raises his voice.*)   If there's anyone in the
house thinks he's fit to take a fall out of Adolphus Grigson—(*tapping
his chest*) he's here—a man ; they'll find Grigson's no soft thing !

MRS. GRIGSON (*tearfully*).   Dolphie, dear, poor Mr. Davoren wants
to go to bed.

(GRIGSON, *when he hears the name of* DAVOREN, *drunkenly looks round
    room ; sees, in a vague way,* DAVOREN *sitting on* R. *side of bed,* L.,
    and stumbles over to him and stands shakily to DAVOREN'S R.
    DAVOREN *thinks it best to humour* GRIGSON, *but only wishes to get
    him away out of the room.*)

ADOLPHUS GRIGSON (*stumbling towards* DAVOREN).   Davoren ?
He's a man. (*Holding out his hand to* DAVOREN.)   Leave it there,
mate. (DAVOREN *shakes hands with him.*)   You needn't be afraid
of Adolphus Grigson ; there never was a dhrop of informer's blood
in the whole family of Grigsons.   I don't know what you are, or
what you think, but you're a man (*loudly*), an' not like some of the
gougers in this house, that ud hang you !

(GRIGSON *crosses from bed,* L., *to bed,* R., *and bends down over*
    SEUMAS.)

(*To* SEUMAS.)   Not referrin' to you, Mr. Shields.

MRS. GRIGSON (*near door,* R., *looking at* SEUMAS).   Oh, you're not
deludin' to Mr. Shields.

SEUMAS (*placatingly, to* GRIGSON).   I know that, Mr. Grigson ;
go on down, now, with Mrs. Grigson, an' have a little sleep.

Adolphus Grigson (*importantly*). I tie myself to no woman's apron strings, Mr. Shields. I know how to keep Mrs. Grigson in her place ; I have the authority of the Bible for that.

(*He goes unsteadily from the bed where* Seumas *is, to the bed*, l. *on which* Davoren *is sitting, and speaks to him confidentially, to* Davoren's *annoyance.*)

(*To* Davoren.)   I know the Bible from cover to cover, Mr. Davoren, an' that's more than some in this house could say. An' what does the Holy Scripture say about woman ?   It says " the woman shall be subject to her husband," an' I'll see that Mrs. Grigson keeps the teachin' of the holy book in the letther an' in the spirit. (*Confidentially bending down over* Davoren. *To* Davoren.) If you're ever in throuble, Mr. Davoren, an' Grigson can help, I'm your man —have you me ?

Davoren.   I have you, Mr. Grigson, I have you.

Adolphus Grigson (*upright again*). Right. I'm an Orangeman ; but I'm not ashamed of it, an' I'm not afraid of it ; but I can feel for a true man, all the same.

(*He wanders over to the head of bed where Shields is, and stoops over him.*)

Have you got me, Mr. Shields ?

Seumas (*humouring* Grigson). Oh, we know you well, Mr. Grigson. Many a true Irishman was a Protestant—Tone, Emmet, Parnell——

Adolphus Grigson (*interrupting*). Mind you, I'm not sayin' as I agree with them you've mentioned, for the Bible forbids it, an' Adolphus Grigson'll always abide by the Bible. Fear God an' honour the king—that's written in Holy Scripture, an' there's no blottin' it out.

(*He staggers over from the bed where* Seumas *is, to the bed on which* Davoren *is sitting, and pulls a pint bottle of whisky from his breast pocket, and taking out the cork, offers the bottle to* Davoren.)

But, now, Mr. Davoren, have a dhrink—just to show there's no coolness.

Davoren (*refusing*). No, no, Mr. Grigson ; it's too late now to take anything. Go on down with Mrs. Grigson, and we can have a chat in the morning.

Adolphus Grigson. Sure you won't have a drink ?

Davoren. Quite sure—thanks all the same.

Adolphus Grigson (*drinking*). Here's the first to-day ! To all true men, even if they were born in a bottle. Here's to King William, to the battle av the Boyne ; to the Hobah Black Chapter —that's my Lodge, Mr. Davoren ; an' to The Orange Lily O. (*Singing in a loud shout*) :

An' dud ya go to see the show, each rose an' pinkadilly O,
To feast your eyes an' view the prize won be the Orange Lily O
The Vic'roy there, so debonair, just like a daffadilly O,
With Lady Clarke, blithe as a lark, approached the Orange Lily O.

> Heigh Ho the Lily O,
> The Royal, Loyal Lily O,
Beneath the sky what flower can vie with Erin's Orange Lily O.

DAVOREN (*in agony*). Holy God, isn't this terrible !

(*In the distance is heard the sound of an engine in an approaching
    motor-car ; the sound faint at first, gradually gets louder.*)

ADOLPHUS GRIGSON (*singing jubilantly*). The elated Muse, to
    hear the news, jumped like a Connaught filly O,
As gossip Fame did loud proclaim, the triumph av the Lily O.
The Lowland field may roses yield, gay heaths the Highlands hilly
    O ;
But high or low no flower can show like Erin's Orange Lily O.
> Heigh Ho the Lily O,
> The Royal, Loyal Lily O,
Beneath the sky what flower can vie with Erin's Or . . .

(*On the second line of the song the sound of the engine has become clear.
    All but* GRIGSON *listen intently,* SEUMAS *gradually rising in the bed
    on to his elbow, his gaze going towards the window. On the third or
    fourth line,* GRIGSON *begins to notice the sound, and the listening
    attitude of the others. He tries to keep bravely on, but, frightened,
    his song trails away to a whisper, and finally stops altogether.*
    DAVOREN *gets up from bed,* L., *comes down to table, and begins to go
    through the papers on the table feverishly.*)

(*With a tremor in his voice.*) There's no need to be afraid, they
couldn't be comin' here.

MRS. GRIGSON (*anxiously*). God forbid ! It ud be terrible if
they came at this hour ov the night.

SEUMAS (*sitting up in bed*). You never know now, Mrs. Grigson ;
they'd rush in on you when you'd be least expectin' them. What,
in the name o' God, is goin' to come out of it all ? Nobody now
cares a traneen about the orders of the Ten Commandments ; the
only order that anybody minds now is, " put your hands up." Oh,
it's a hopeless country.

ADOLPHUS GRIGSON. Whisht ; do you hear them talking outside
at the door ? You're sure of your life nowhere now ; it's just as
safe to go everywhere as it is to anywhere. An' they don't give a
damn whether you're a loyal man or not. If you're a Republican
they make you sing " God save the King," an' if you're loyal they'll
make you sing the " Soldiers' Song." The singin' ud be all right if
they didn't make you dance afterwards.

MRS. GRIGSON. They'd hardly come here unless they heard something about Mr. Davoren.

DAVOREN. About me ! What could they hear about me ?

ADOLPHUS GRIGSON (*viciously*). You'll never get some people to keep their mouths shut. I was in the Blue Lion this evening, an' who do you think was there, blowin' out av him, but that little blower, Tommy Owens ; there he was tellin' everybody that *he* knew where there was bombs ; that *he* had a friend that was a General in the I.R.A. ; that *he* could tell them what the Staff was thinkin' av doin' ; that *he* could lay his hand on tons av revolvers ; that they wasn't a mile from where he was livin', but that *he* knew his own know, an' would keep it to himself.

SEUMAS (*with fierce and venomous energy*). Well, God blast the little blower, anyway ; it's the like ov him that deserves to be plugged ! (*To* DAVOREN.) What are you lookin' for among the books, Donal ?

DAVOREN (*searching among papers on table*). A letter that I got to-day from Mr. Gallogher and Mrs. Henderson ; I'm blessed if I know where I put it.

SEUMAS (*peevishly*). Can't you look for it in the mornin' ?

DAVOREN (*agitated*). It's addressed to the Irish Republican Army, and, considering the possibility of a raid, it would be safer to get rid of it.

(*Shots again heard out in the lane, followed by loud shouts of " Halt, halt, halt ! "*)

ADOLPHUS GRIGSON. I think we had better be gettin' to bed, Debby ; it's not right to be keepin' Mr. Davoren an' Mr. Shields awake.

SEUMAS. An' what made them give you such a letter as that ; don't they know the state the country is in ? An' you were worse to take it. Have you got it ?

(GRIGSON *crosses from* C. *to* MRS. GRIGSON, C.R., *who takes his arm.*)

ADOLPHUS GRIGSON (*going towards door,* R.). Good night, Mr. Davoren ; good night, Mr. Shields.

MRS. GRIGSON (*going with* GRIGSON). Good night, Mr. Shields ; good night, Mr. Davoren.

(*They go out by door,* R. DAVOREN *takes no notice of the departure, but continues to search through the papers frantically.*)

DAVOREN (*in great agitation*). I can't find it anywhere—isn't it terrible !

SEUMAS (*half-out of bed, with eyes staring over at* DAVOREN). What were you thinkin' of when you took such a letter as that ? Ye gods, has nobody any brains at all, at all ? Oh, this is a hopeless country. Did you try in your pockets ?

DAVOREN (*searching in his pockets*).   Oh, thanks be to God, here it is.

SEUMAS.   Burn it now, an', for God's sake, don't take any letters like that again. . . .

(*A pause as the letter is burned by* DAVOREN *over the candle.* SEUMAS *listening.   The sound of the motor engine grows fainter and, finally, dies away.* SEUMAS *lies back on the bed with a deep sigh of relief.*)

There's the motor gone away now, an' we can sleep in peace for the rest of the night.   Just to make sure of everything now, have a look in that bag o' Maguire's : not that there can be anything in it.

DAVOREN.   If there's nothing in it, what's the good of looking ?

SEUMAS.   It won't kill you to look, will it ?

(DAVOREN *goes from back of table to the bed where* SEUMAS *is, takes the bag, left by* MAGUIRE, *from under the bed, carries it back to table, places it there, opens it, and with face pale and eyes staring, starts back.* SEUMAS *watches him in terror.*)

DAVOREN (*shaking with fear*).   My God, it's full of bombs, Mills bombs !

(SEUMAS *climbs on to his knees in the bed, grips the head rails with his hands, and looks over at* DAVOREN, *terrorstricken.*)

SEUMAS.   Holy Mother o' God, you're jokin' !

DAVOREN (*with savage fear*).   If the Tans come, you'll find whether I'm jokin' or no.

SEUMAS.   Oh, isn't this a nice pickle to be in !   (*Losing power of thought.*)   St. Anthony, look down on us.

DAVOREN (*trying to blame* SEUMAS).   There's no use of blaming St. Anthony—why did you let Maguire leave the bag here ?

SEUMAS (*indignant at being blamed*).   Why did I let him leave the bag here ; why did I let him leave the bag here !   How did I know what was in it ?   Didn't I think there was nothin' in it but spoons an' hairpins.   What'll we do now ; what'll we do now ?   Mother o' God, grant there'll be no raid to-night.   I knew things ud go wrong when I missed Mass this mornin'.

(DAVOREN, *in a panic of rage, goes over to* SEUMAS *and stands over him, head of bed,* R.)

DAVOREN (*fiercely*).   Give over your prayin', an' let us think of what is best to be done.

(*He walks up and down between beds.*)

There's one thing certain—as soon as morning comes, I'm on the run out of this house.

SEUMAS (*with angry scorn*).   Thinkin' of yourself, like the rest of them.   Leavin' me to bear the brunt of it.

DAVOREN.   And why shouldn't you bear the brunt of it ?

Maguire was no friend of mine ; besides, it's your fault ; you knew the sort of a man he was, and you should have been on your guard.

SEUMAS.   Did I know he was a gunman ; did I know he was a gunman ; did I know he was a gunman ? Did . . .

DAVOREN.   Do you mean to tell me that . . .

SEUMAS.   Just a moment . . .

DAVOREN.   You didn't know . . .

SEUMAS.   Just a moment . . .

DAVOREN.   That Maguire was connected with . . .

SEUMAS (*loudly*).   Just a moment ; can't . . .

DAVOREN.   The Republican Movement ? What's the use of trying to tell damn lies !

(MINNIE POWELL *rushes into the room. She is only partly dressed, and has thrown a shawl over her shoulders. She is in a state of intense excitement.*)

MINNIE (*dashing from door*, R., *over to* DAVOREN, *sitting helpless and almost fainting on* R. *side of bed*, L.). Donal, Mr. Davoren, they're all round the house ! They must be goin' to raid the place ; I was lookin' out of the window an' I seen them. I do be on the watch every night.

(*She dashes to window*, C. *back, looks out through the curtains ; then turns back to look at* DAVOREN.)

Have you anything—if you have . . .

(*There is heard at street door a violent and continuous knocking, followed by the crash of glass and the beating of the door with rifle butts.*)

There they are, there they are, there they are !

(DAVOREN *reclines almost fainting on the bed ;* SEUMAS *sits up in an attitude of agonized prayerfulness ;* MINNIE *alone retains her presence of mind. When she sees their panic she becomes calm, though her words are rapidly spoken, and her actions are performed with decisive celerity.*)

(*Leaving window, returning to* DAVOREN's *side, talking with precision and great quickness.*) What is it ; what have you got ; where is it !

DAVOREN (*faintly, to* MINNIE).   Bombs, bombs, bombs ; my God, in the bag on the table there—we're done, we're done !

SEUMAS.   Holy St. Anthony, do you hear them battherin' at the door !

(*A heavy crash of breaking glass heard outside.*)

(*Prostrate.*)   There's the glass gone—say an act of contrition, Donal.

(MINNIE *goes from* DAVOREN *to the table, shuts bag and takes it in her arms.*)

MINNIE. I'll take them to my room ; maybe they won't search it ; if they do, aself, they won't harm a girl.

(MINNIE, *carrying the bag carefully goes to door,* R. ; *at door she turns, looking towards* DAVOREN.)

(*Glancing lovingly at* DONAL.) Good-bye . . . Donal !

(*She hurries out by door,* R.)

SEUMAS. If we come through this I'll never miss a Mass again ! If it's the Tommies, it won't be so bad, but if it's the Tans, we're goin' to have a terrible time.

(*The street door is broken open and heavy steps are heard in the hall, punctuated with shouts of "'Old the light 'ere," "Put 'em up," etc. An* AUXILIARY *opens the door of the room and enters, revolver in one hand and electric torch in the other.*)

THE AUXILIARY. 'Oo's 'ere ?
SEUMAS (*as if he didn't know*). Who—who's that ?
THE AUXILIARY (*peremptorily*). 'Oo's 'ere ?
SEUMAS (*humbly*). Only two men, sir, me an' me mate in the other bed.

(THE AUXILIARY *comes into the room cautiously, moves his torch so that the light falls on the face of* SEUMAS ; *he comes over angrily to* SEUMAS *and stands beside him.*)

THE AUXILIARY. Why didn't you open the door ?
SEUMAS (*with respectful assurance*). We didn't hear you knockin', sir.
THE AUXILIARY (*ironically*). You must be a little 'ard of 'earing, eh ?
SEUMAS (*sorrowfully*). I had rheumatic fever a few years ago, an' ever since I do be—I do be a little hard of hearin'.

(THE AUXILIARY *flashes light of torch on* DAVOREN *sitting* R. *side of bed,* L., *and goes over to him.*)

THE AUXILIARY (*to* DAVOREN). 'Ow is it you're not in bed ?
DAVOREN (*submissively*). I was in bed, but when I heard the knockin', I got up to open the door.
THE AUXILIARY (*scornfully*). You're a kind blowke, you are. Delighted, like, to have a visit from us, eh ?

(DAVOREN *remains silent.*)

(*Threatening to strike him with revolver.*) Why downt you answer !
DAVOREN. Yes, sir.
THE AUXILIARY (*indicating bed*). Up on the bed, quick.

(DAVOREN *springs up on the bed,* L.)

Put them up—quick !

(DAVOREN *puts his hands over his head.* THE AUXILIARY *carefully taps the trouser pockets of* DONAL. *When he has done so, he looks at him, and keeps him covered with revolver.*)

What's your name ?

DAVOREN. Davoren, Dan Davoren, sir.

THE AUXILIARY. You're not an Irishman, are you ?

DAVOREN. I—I—I was born in Ireland.

THE AUXILIARY. Ow, you were, were you ; Irish han' proud of it, ay ? (*With nod to* DAVOREN.) Stand down . . . Put 'em down.

(DAVOREN *steps down from bed, and takes down his hands.* THE AUXILIARY *goes over to foot of bed* R., *and stands facing* SEUMAS, *while keeping an eye on* DAVOREN.)

(*Ominously, to* SEUMAS.) What's your name ?

SEUMAS. Seuma . . . Oh no ; Jimmie Shields, sir.

THE AUXILIARY. Ow, you're a selt (*he means a Celt*), one of the seltic race that speaks a lingo of its ahn, and that's going to overthrow the British Empire—I don't think ! 'Ere, where's your gun ?

SEUMAS. I never had a gun in me hand in me life.

THE AUXILIARY. No ; you wouldn't know what a gun was, if you saw one, I suppose ?

(THE AUXILIARY *shoves his revolver under the nose of* SEUMAS.)

'Ere, what's this ?

SEUMAS (*in a sweat of fear*). Oh, be careful, please be careful.

THE AUXILIARY (*carelessly*). Why, what 'ave I got to be careful abaht ?

SEUMAS (*protestingly*). The gun—it, it, it, might go off !

THE AUXILIARY. An' what price if it did ? It can easily be reloaded.

(*He replaces revolver in holster. He goes across room between beds, to back, and comes to dresser.*)

(*Looking at dresser.*) Waht's in this press ? Any ammunition in 'ere ?

(*He opens bottom part of dresser and throws out a few old papers and clothes that are in it.*)

SEUMAS (*in a whisper of fear*). Only a bit of grub, sir. You'll get nothing there ; no one in this house has any connection with politics.

THE AUXILIARY (*looking at* SEUMAS). No ? I've never met a man yet that didn't say that ; but we're a little bit too ikey now to be kidded with that sort of talk.

SEUMAS (*appealingly to* THE AUXILIARY). May I go an' get a drink of water ?

The Auxiliary. You'll want a barrel of water before you're done with us.

(The Auxiliary *crosses from dresser down* L. *to fireplace. He glances at mantelpiece and sees statues.*)

'Ello, what's ere ? A statue of Christ. And a crucifix ! Think you was in a bloomin' monastery.

(The Auxiliary *begins to examine papers on table. Looking at them and as he finds them harmless, scattering them on the floor.*)

(Mrs. Grigson, *very excited, enters by door* R.)

Mrs. Grigson. They're turning the place upside down. Upstairs an' downstairs they're makin' a litter of everything ! I declare to God, it's awful what law-abidin' people have to put up with. An' they found a pint bottle of whisky under Dolphie's pillow, an' they're drinkin' every drop of it—an' Dolphie 'll be like a devil in the mornin' when he finds he has no curer.

(The Auxiliary, *who has lifted his head at the mention of whisky, rushes across to* Mrs. Grigson *and catches her arm.*)

The Auxiliary. A bottle of whisky, ay ? 'Ere, where do you live—quick, where do you live ?

Mrs. Grigson. Down in the kitchen—an' when you go down, will you ask them not to drink—(*she looks after* The Auxiliary, *door,* R.)—oh, he's gone without listenin' to me.

(*While* Mrs. Grigson *is speaking* The Auxiliary *rushes out.*)

Seumas (*anxiously to* Mrs. Grigson *who comes back just inside door,* R.). Are they searchin' the whole house, Mrs. Grigson ?

Mrs. Grigson. They didn't leave a thing in the kitchen that they didn't flitter about the floor ; the things in the cupboard, all the little odds an' ends that I keep in the big box, an . . .

Seumas. Oh, they're a terrible gang of blaguards—did they go upstairs ?—they'd hardly search Minnie Powell's room—do you think, would they, Mrs. Grigson ?

Mrs. Grigson. Just to show them the sort of a man he was, before they come in, Dolphie put the big Bible on the table, open at the First Gospel of St. Peter, second chapter, an' marked the thirteenth to the seventeenth verse in red ink—you know the passages, Mr. Shields—(*quoting*): " Submit yourselves to every ordinance of man for the Lord's sake. . . . Love the brotherhood. Fear God. Honour the King." (*Coming over close to* Seumas.) An' what do you think they did, Mr. Shields ? They caught a hold of the Bible an' flung it on the floor—imagine that, Mr. Shields—flingin' the Bible on the floor ! Then one of them says to another—" Jack," says he, " have you seen the light ; is your soul saved ? " An' then they grabbed hold of poor Dolphie, callin' him Mr. Moody an' Mr. Sankey, an' wanted him to offer up a prayer for the Irish Republic ! An' when they were puttin' me out, there they had the poor man sittin' up in bed, his hands crossed on his breast, his eyes lookin' up at the ceilin', an' he singin' a hymn—" We shall meet in the Sweet Bye an' Bye "—an' all the time, Mr. Shields, there they were drinkin' his whisky ; there's torture for you, an' they all laughin' at poor Dolphie's terrible sufferin's.

DAVOREN (to MRS. GRIGSON). In the name of all that's sensible, what did he want to bring whisky home with him for ? They're bad enough sober, what'll they be like when they're drunk ?

MRS. GRIGSON (plaintively). He always brings a drop home with him—he calls it his medicine.

SEUMAS (still anxious). They'll hardly search all the house ; do you think they will, Mrs. Grigson ?

MRS. GRIGSON. An' we have a picture over the mantelpiece of King William crossing the Boyne, an' do you know what they wanted to make out, Mr. Shields, that it was Robert Emmet, an' the picture of a sacret society !

(MRS. GRIGSON wanders out of room by door, R.)

SEUMAS (maddened by her inattention to what he says). She's not listenin' to a word I'm sayin' ! Oh, the country is hopeless an' the people is hopeless.

DAVOREN. For God's sake tell her to go to hell out of this—she's worse than the Auxsie.

SEUMAS (thoughtfully). Let her stay where she is ; it's safer to have a woman in the room. If they come across the bombs I hope to God Minnie 'll say nothin'.

DAVOREN. We're a pair of pitiable cowards to let poor Minnie suffer when we know that we and not she are to blame.

SEUMAS. What else can we do, man ? Do you want us to be done in ? If you're anxious to be riddled, I'm not. Besides, they won't harm her, she's only a girl, an' so long as she keeps her mouth shut it'll be all right.

DAVOREN. I wish I could be sure of that.

(MRS. GRIGSON wanders in again, by door, R., and stands shakily near the bed where SEUMAS is.)

SEUMAS. D'ye think are they goin', Mrs. Grigson ? What are they doin' now ?

MRS. GRIGSON (who is standing at the door, looking out into the hall). There's not a bit of me that's not shakin' like a jelly !

SEUMAS. Are they gone upstairs, Mrs. Grigson ? Do you think, Mrs. Grigson, will they soon be goin' ?

MRS. GRIGSON. When they were makin' poor Dolphie sit up in the bed, I 'clare to God I thought every minute I'd hear their guns goin' off, an' see poor Dolphie stretched out dead in the bed— whisht, God bless us, I think I hear him moanin' !

SEUMAS. You might as well be talking to a stone ! They're all hopeless, hopeless, hopeless! She thinks she hears him moanin'. It's bloody near time somebody made him moan!

DAVOREN (*with a sickly attempt at humour*). He's moaning for the loss of his whisky.

(*A definite commotion, movement of persons and their voices outside door*, R. *Loud and angry commands of " Go on," " Get out and get into the lorry," are heard, mingled with a girl's voice—it is* MINNIE'S *—shouting bravely, but a little hysterically, " Up the Republic.")*

MRS. GRIGSON (*from the door*). God save us, they're takin' Minnie, they're takin' Minnie Powell! (*Running out.*) What in the name of God can have happened?

SEUMAS. Holy Saint Anthony grant that she'll keep her mouth shut.

DAVOREN (*sitting down on the bed and covering his face with his hands*). We'll never again be able to lift up our heads if anything happens to Minnie.

(SEUMAS *sits up in bed and looks appealingly at* DAVOREN.)

SEUMAS. For God's sake keep quiet or somebody'll hear you; nothin'll happen to her, nothin' at all—it'll be all right if she only keeps her mouth shut.

MRS. GRIGSON (*running in by door*, R.). They're after gettin' a whole lot of stuff in Minnie's room! Enough to blow up the whole street, a Tan says! God to-night, who'd have ever thought that of Minnie Powell!

(MRS. GRIGSON *crosses between beds, to back, and looks out of window*, C., *back.*)

SEUMAS. Did she say anything, is she sayin' anything, what's she sayin', Mrs. Grigson?

MRS. GRIGSON. She's shoutin' "Up the Republic" at the top of her voice. An' big Mrs. Henderson is fightin' with the soldiers —she's after nearly knockin' one of them down, an' they're puttin' her into the lorry too.

SEUMAS (*venomously*). God blast her! Can she not mind her own business? What does she want here—didn't she know there was a raid on? Is the whole damn country goin' mad! They'll open fire in a minute an' innocent people'll be shot!

DAVOREN (*anxiously*). What way are they using Minnie, Mrs. Grigson; are they rough with her?

MRS. GRIGSON (*angrily*). They couldn't be half-rough enough; the little hussy, to be so deceitful; she might as well have had the house blew up! God to-night, who'd think it was in Minnie Powell!

SEUMAS. Oh, grant she won't say anything!

MRS. GRIGSON. There they're goin' away, now; ah, then I hope they'll give that Minnie Powell a coolin'.

SEUMAS (*fervently*). God grant she won't say anything! Are they gone, Mrs. Grigson?

Mrs. Grigson. With her fancy stockins, an' her pom-poms, an' her crêpe de chine blouses ! I knew she'd come to no good !

Seumas (*to* Mrs. Grigson). Are they gone, Mrs. Grigson ?

Mrs. Grigson. They're gone, Mr. Shields.

(Adolphus Grigson *enters airily by door,* r. *He is wearing trousers, shirt and socks.*)

(*Seeing* Grigson.) Here's poor Dolphie, an' not a feather asthray on him. (*Running over* r. *to meet him.*) Oh, Dolphie, dear. you're all right, thanks to God—I thought you'd never see the mornin' !

Adolphus Grigson (*airily*). Of course I'm all right ; what ud put a bother on Dolphie Grigson ?—not the Tans anyway !

Mrs. Grigson. When I seen you stretched out on the bed, an' you . . . singin' a hymn . . .

Adolphus Grigson (*fearful of possible humiliatinn*). Who was singin' a hymn ? When did you hear me singin' a hymn ? D'ye hear me talkin' to you—where did you hear me singin' a hymn ?

Mrs. Grigson. I was only jokin', Dolphie, dear ; I . . .

Adolphus Grigson (*furious*). You're place is below, an' not gosterin' here to men ; down with you quick !

(*He pushes her towards door,* r. *and* Mrs. Grigson *hurriedly leaves the room.*)

(*Nonchalantly taking out his pipe, filling it, lighting it, and beginning to smoke, standing* c. *between beds.*) Excitin' few moments, Mr. Davoren ; Mrs. G. lost her head completely—panic-stricken. But that's only natural, all woman is very nervous. The only thing to do is to show them that they can't put the wind up you ; show the least sign of fright an' they'd walk on you, simply walk on you. Two of them come down—" Put them up," revolvers under your nose—you know, the usual way. " What's all the bother about ? " says I, quite calm. " No bother at all," says one of them, " only this gun might go off an' hit somebody—have you me ? " says he. " What if it does," says I, " a man can only die once, an' you'll find Grigson won't squeal." " God, you're a cool one," says the other, " there's no blottin' it out."

Seumas (*calm and confident again*). That's the best way to take them ; it only makes things worse to show that you've got the wind up. " Any ammunition here ? " says the fellow that come in here. " I don't think so," says I, " but you better have a look. " No back talk," says he, " or you might get plugged." " I don't know of any clause," says I, " in the British Constitution that makes it a crime for a man to speak in his own room,"—with that, he just had a look round, an' off he went.

Adolphus Grigson. If a man keeps a stiff upper front—Merciful God, there's an ambush !

(*Explosions of two bursting bombs are heard on the street outside the house, followed by fierce and rapid revolver and rifle fire. People are*

heard rushing into the hall, and there is general clamour and confusion.
SEUMAS *and* DAVOREN *cower down in the room ;* GRIGSON, *after a few moments' hesitation, frankly rushes out of the room to what he conceives to be the safer asylum of the kitchen. A lull follows, punctuated by an odd rifle-shot ; then comes a peculiar and ominous stillness, broken in a few moments by the sounds of voices and movement. Questions are heard, outside door,* R., *being asked :* " Who was it was killed ? " " Where was she shot ? " *which are answered by* " MINNIE POWELL " ; " She went to jump off the lorry an' she was shot." " She's not dead, is she ? " " They say she's dead— shot through the buzzum ! ")*

DAVOREN (*in a tone of horror-stricken doubt standing up rigidly*). D'ye hear what they're sayin', Shields, d'ye hear what they're sayin' ?—Minnie Powell is shot.

SEUMAS (*panic-stricken*). For God's sake speak easy, an' don't bring them in here on top of us again.

DAVOREN. Is that all you're thinking of ? Do you realize that she has been shot to save us ?

SEUMAS. Is it my fault ; am I to blame ?

DAVOREN. It is your fault and mine, both ; oh, we're a pair of dastardly cowards to have let her do what she did.

SEUMAS. She did it off her own bat—we didn't ask her to do it.

(MRS. GRIGSON *enters. She is excited and semi-hysterical, and sincerely affected by the tragic occurrence.*)

MRS. GRIGSON (*standing between beds*). What's goin' to happen next ! Oh, Mr. Davoren, isn't it terrible, isn't it terrible ! Minnie Powell, poor little Minnie Powell's been shot dead ! They were raidin' a house a few doors down, an' had just got up in their lorries to go away when they was ambushed. You never heard such shootin' ! An' in the thick of it, poor Minnie went to jump off the lorry she was on, an' she was shot through the buzzum. Oh, it was horrible to see the blood pourin' out, an' Minnie moanin'. They found some paper in her breast, with " Minnie " written on it, an' some other name they couldn't make out with the blood ; the officer kep' it. The ambulance is bringin' her to the hospital, but what good's that when she's dead ! Poor little Minnie, poor little Minnie Powell, to think of you full of life a few minutes ago, an' now she's dead !

DAVOREN. Ah me, alas ! Pain, pain, pain ever, for ever ! It's terrible to think that little Minnie is dead, but it's still more terrible to think that Davoren and Shields are alive ! Oh, Donal Davoren, shame is your portion now till the silver cord is loosened and the golden bowl be broken. Oh, Davoren, Donal Davoren, poet and poltroon, poltroon and poet !

SEUMAS (*solemnly lying flat on back in bed*). I knew something ud come of the tappin' on the wall !

CURTAIN.

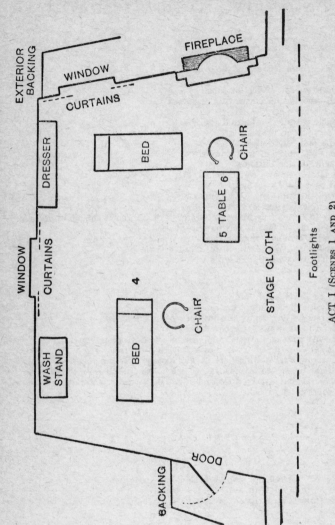

ACT I (SCENES 1 AND 2)

4. Suitcase. 5. Vase of Wild Flowers. 6. Typewriter.

PROPERTY AND FURNITURE PLOT

ACT I

Dresser with crockery.
Two single beds.
Fireplace with fender and fittings.
Small table.
Typewriter, and paper for same.
Small crucifix and statue of the Sacred Heart
Two kitchen chairs.
Washhand stand, basin and jug.
Jug of milk on dresser.
Candle and candlestick.
Vase with bunch of wild flowers.
Big suitcase for SHIELDS.
Packages of spoons, forks, braces, etc.
Rent-book for LANDLORD.
Two Notices to Quit for LANDLORD.
Small milk jug for MINNIE.
Letter to be read by MR. GALLOGHER—this document should be as small as
    possible so that it can be burned easily.
Pen for DAVOREN, which GALLOGHER uses.
Notebook and pencil stump for TOMMY OWENS.
Bag full of bombs for MAGUIRE.

ACT II

Same as Act I, with addition of,
Revolver and cartridges for shots off.
Revolver, holster, and torch for THE AUXILIARY.
Pint bottle of whisky for GRIGSON.
Note.—AUXILIARY. Auxie's uniform is black trousers, no leggings, black,
    tightly buttoned coat, brown leather belt, from which hang two long
    narrow straps, which are caught loosely by strap round upper part of
    right thigh ; to this is attached the holster, and it is on the thigh so that
    the revolver can be drawn rapidly. He wears a black Balmoral cap with
    short black ribbons.

LIGHTING PLOT

ACT I

Floats (white) full up. No. 1 batten full up, white.
Four white lamp strip over window-back.
Four white lamp strip on door, R.

ACT II

Strip at door out.
Strip at window out.
Blue floats, half-up. Frosted baby amber shot on candle.
Steel-blue flood through window, above fireplace, L., directed on to head of
    bed of SHIELDS.